daring to dream
Women Succeeding through Education

Sue Lawrence
Suzi Wong

EDITORS

d

Hill Street Press
Athens, Georgia

A HILL STREET PRESS BOOK

Published in the United States of America by

Hill Street Press LLC
191 E Broad Street | Suite 216
Athens, Georgia 30601 USA
www.hillstreetpress.com

Hill Street Press is committed to preserving the written word. Every
effort is made to print books on acid-free paper with a significant
amount of post-consumer recycled content.

Printed in the United States of America.

Library of Congress Cataloging-in-Publication data on file. Please
contact the publisher.

ISBN 978-1-58818-132-9

9 8 7 6 5 4 3 2 1
First Printing

This book is dedicated to all women who aspire to build better lives through education, and especially to the Jeannette Rankin Foundation Scholars. Further, it is dedicated to all those who help others achieve their dreams by giving time and treasure to provide the greatest gift: the gift of hope for a future of dignity, love, and peace.

=

table of contents

foreword

Five years ago, I had the privilege of flying a very significant historic artifact during one of my missions to the International Space Station. It was a banner of the National Women's Party, used early in the 20th century as the party fought to secure for women the most basic right of a democracy, the right to vote. Women's suffrage provided a greater representation of diverse views in our political and social system, an important milestone that eventually led to NASA's selection of the first six women astronauts in 1978. Twenty years later, my third space mission included three women astronauts as part of the crew, and I was proud to carry that banner in honor of all of the women who had come before us.

It's interesting to look back at what the press wrote about the shuttle program not long before the first launch over 20 years ago. In one newspaper, it said, "the shuttle is supposed to be able to retrieve satellites and bring them back to Earth, but it can't. It flat out, simply cannot." And yet, the shuttle did just that within a few years—deploying satellites, retrieving them from orbit, repairing them and redeploying them. Thank goodness the people at NASA didn't listen to that writer and didn't cancel the whole program. The easier path is always to go along with the skeptics and those who say it will never work or never make a difference. But it's infinitely more rewarding to try to prove them wrong.

Almost everyone needs support and encouragement, and I'm certainly no exception. My mother encouraged all of my brothers and sisters and I to pursue a good education, and that helped motivate me to go to college. Once at college, although I was interested in many subjects and I did well in classes, I really had no idea of what I wanted to do. When I was growing up, there were no scientists or engineers in my family to describe to me what their careers were like. It was only after I'd changed my major five times in college, going through music and business among others, that I ended up in Physics, and that was primarily due to a professor who encouraged me after I'd done well in one of his classes.

So by the time I graduated from college I had unknowingly made two very good decisions necessary for the astronaut program: first, to get a college education, and second, to major in a technical field. The first I can attribute to my mother's interest in education and her encouragement of all of my brothers and sisters and me to pursue a good education. She didn't have an opportunity to go to college when she was young, but she was always interested in learning, and she began taking college courses one at a time as she was raising five children. She finally graduated from college two years after I did!

As for majoring in a technical field: it came out pretty much by accident. I became interested in physics partly through math class—when I realized I was one of the few people taking them for fun instead of to fulfill their major requirements. I noticed that everyone else in the math classes had some idea of what the equations we were solving meant in the physical world, so I wanted to find out too.

An advisor in the electrical engineering department was discouraging—he noted that a woman had "come through the program once" and talked about how difficult it was, without ever checking to see what kind of student I was or what math I had taken. In contrast, the physics department advisor told me about a number of interesting career paths one could take with a degree in physics, was delighted to find out I had already finished the calculus series, and said he thought I would do very well. It's not too surprising that I chose physics!

When I was at Stanford for graduate school, I heard about the astronaut program from some friends who were applying. I had never considered it before because it never occurred to me that I would get to a position in my life where I might be qualified. I wrote and found out the basic qualifications were a college degree in science and engineering, which I had, and either work experience or a graduate degree, which I was in the process of getting. I realized that I was at least eligible to apply. However, I was realistic; I figured I had almost no chance of ever being selected, and I continued pursuing my Ph.D. toward my previous goal of a career in research engineering. As soon as I finished my doctorate, I sent my application in. About two years later, NASA held its selection round, and I spent a week interviewing for their next class of astronauts. Although I wasn't chosen that year, I realized that I actually had a chance of making it some day.

The sense of camaraderie and of purpose in the Astronaut Office was very evident. At that time, they were recovering from Challenger accident and were very focused on returning to flight. It also became clear to me that determination/perseverance was very important – many of the people selected that year had applied and interviewed several times over a period of 10 years. That was certainly not seen as a drawback by NASA, in fact quite the opposite; they want to make sure they select people who haven't applied on a whim or without carefully considering exactly what the job will be like, and who are willing to work hard toward a goal over many years.

So I decided to do whatever I could to increase my

chances of making it in the next selection. I was fortunate to work with excellent people both at Stanford and at Sandia National laboratories. I was a co-inventor on three patents during that time and published several papers in technical journals. I also took the opportunity to learn to fly and received my pilot's license.

I became convinced that I wanted to work for NASA even if I was never selected as an astronaut. I moved to NASA Ames Research Center in California to head their optics research group and soon after became branch chief of an advanced computing research group. Three years later, when the next astronaut selection rolled around, I was one of the lucky twenty-three people chosen to join the astronaut corps. It's been an incredibly rewarding fourteen years, and of course the highlights are my space missions.

My first flights studied atmospheric chemistry and particularly the problem of ozone depletion as part of NASA's Mission to Planet Earth program. My next flights were part of the assembly of the International Space Station, during which we transferred supplies to prepare for the first crew to live onboard, and later added a major piece of truss equipment. I was fortunate to operate both the shuttle and station robot arms during those flights, to help install the truss, and to move spacewalking crewmembers around to assist in their assembly tasks.

The most rewarding part of my job is the chance to work closely with incredibly talented people. To take a group of individuals from different backgrounds and often different countries and to build them into a smoothly operating team creates a degree of camaraderie and friendship that is hard to explain.

Too often, as we who work at NASA know all too well, you hear only from those who are always willing to criticize or to provide discouragement in whatever you may try. Today's space program is truly a place where women and men from around the world bring their strengths and commitment together to achieve a shared vision. It may seem difficult or scary to pursue ambitious goals, but realize that you don't have to do it alone.

In fact, the Jeannette Rankin Foundation is set up to show women that they have supporters, people who are willing to help provide others with the training and confidence that they will need to improve their lives and their communities. They help women pursue their educational goals, and not have to "go it alone."

I'm reminded of a quote from sociologist Marshall McLuhan that seems to speak both to our responsibility to utilize knowledge to our best ability and to work together for the benefit of humankind. He said, "There are no passengers on spaceship Earth. We are all crew."

Dr. Ellen Ochoa
June, 2004, JRF Annual Dinner keynote speech

Dr. Ochoa is the first Hispanic female astronaut. She serves as Deputy Director of Lyndon B. Johnson Space Center. During her distinguished service at NASA, she has received numerous honors and recognitions. Her educational background includes a bachelor of science degree in physics from San Diego State University, a master of science degree and a doctorate in electrical engineering from Stanford University. Dr. Ochoa's research at Sandia National Laboratories and NASA Ames Research Center comprised investigations of optical systems for performing information processing and research and development of computational systems for aerospace missions. Her experience includes four space flight missions between 1993 and 2002. Two schools have been named in honor of her: Ellen Ochoa Middle School in Pasco, Washington, and Ellen Ochoa Learning Center in Cudahy, California.

> God grant us the courage and wisdom
> to insist that the abundance we have
> may be shared with all humankind; that
> freedom, justice, righteousness, goodwill,
> and everlasting peace be established
> throughout the world.
>
> — Jeannette Rankin

Introduction

You hold in your hands a book about thirty women whose paths have never crossed but whose stories reveal a special sisterhood. Sometime between 1976 and 2008, each of these women applied for a scholarship from the Jeannette Rankin Foundation in Athens, Georgia. The foundation's mission is to help low-income women age 35 and older succeed through education. These thirty women are among the hundreds who have received JRF scholarships in the past thirty years.

You hold in your hands a book about thirty women who followed their dreams and discovered through education the means to transform their lives. Whether African American or Native American, whether from San Antonio or Santa Cruz, whether aspiring artist or nurse or engineer — each woman tells a compelling story. There is Ardella who was shot in the head at close range. And Sandra who had 90% of her tongue removed because of oral cancer, but received a standing ovation for her commencement speech. And Aree, who emigrated to the U.S. from Thailand. And Sandi, the survivor of six generations of incest and alcoholism, who now has a Ph.D. And Suzunn, who returned to school at age 50 to rebuild her life and later gave back by donating a scholarship to help another woman to go back to college.

You hold in your hands thirty profiles of hope and courage. Each story is remarkable in its own right, but together, they weave a tapestry of emergence and empowerment. Most of these older, non-traditional students are the first in their families to go beyond high school. Many bear the scars of a traumatic childhood: sexual abuse, substance abuse, domestic violence, and poverty. As teens, they had neither financial nor moral support for higher education. Only later in life did each woman seek higher education as the means to breaking generations-long cycles of deprivation, dependence, and diminished possibilities.

Only later in life did they send a scholarship application to Athens, Georgia, headquarters of the Jeannette Rankin Foundation. To this day, women send in these testaments of desperate need and ardent desire. Their budget statements indicate bottom lines of limited incomes and pinched lives, but their personal essays reveal optimism, high goals, and strength of character. In the scholarship applications, obstacles are mentioned, but also the determination to overcome those obstacles.

You hold in your hands thirty stories that prove education is worth every penny invested. With the help of the Jeannette Rankin Foundation scholarship, these women as well as hundreds of others went on to improve not only their own lives, but also the lives of their children and their communities. They met and exceeded their goals. They launched careers and attained economic stability. But, above the material gains, all 30 women treasure the intangible rewards of education: self-esteem, self-confidence, richer cultural and intellectual lives, and an expanded perspective. It is clear that they changed themselves and are making a difference in their world.

As you hold this book in your hands, please also hold these women in your hearts. I met each of them on the page, through words submitted in scholarship applications. Then, I introduced myself on the telephone and conducted interviews across the nation's four time zones. Our conversations were intense — often meandering, often emotional, always affirmative, always rich and rewarding.

With retrospective insight, each woman spoke of the ways in which a relatively small scholarship hugely shaped her life. Each emphasized the transformative power of education. They took me on their journey of expanding horizons and deepening self-awareness. They offered advice, encouragement, and practical wisdom to today's non-traditional women students. They thanked me for the JRF scholarship and most of all, for the vote of confidence they gained just from knowing that absolute strangers believed in them and invested in their potential. I thanked them for their memories and their generosity of spirit. We laughed; we cried.

To be trusted with their stories is an honor and a privilege. I know the scholarship recipients give their heartfelt support to this book and welcome you into a unique sisterhood of phenomenal women. As one scholar said, "Let other women know your story. Your greatest suffering and heartache becomes your greatest gift. How you go through the hard stuff and what you make of it once you come out on the other side will be the source of many blessings."

Suzi Wong
Athens, Georgia
May 2008

"It isn't where you come from; it's where you are going that counts."
—Ella Fitzgerald

"Luck? I don't know anything about luck. I've never banked on it, and I'm afraid of people who do.
Luck to me is something else:
hard work, and realizing what is opportunity and what isn't."
—Lucille Ball

i've Waited long enough

carolyn bushey

"I know what it is like
to grab small children and run
out of the house in
the middle of the night
with only the clothes on your back.
I know what it feels like to be able to
rebuild your life into
one that is safe and happy,
one that is safe for your children."

In my life, I feel my soul has experienced every
dysfunction known to man. I came to a point when I was
in so much pain that it became clear — I might as well turn
around and make some good come of it. That's when I began
rebuilding my spirit and when I dedicated my life to helping
people in the trenches, people who were like I was, a battered
woman, addicted to alcohol, a mother of two small children
living in shame and fear.

3

I know a lot about battered women and abused children. I know what it is like to grab small children and run out of the house in the middle of the night with only the clothes on your back. I know what denial is like, to wake up each morning and hope that it really isn't as bad as it seems. I know how it feels to think you are taking your children's father away from them. I understand the hopelessness of not having enough money to get away, and I know what it feels like to live with shame and fear. I understand the dynamics behind trying to save a marriage because you believe in the vows you took. And I understand what it feels like to be finally broken in body, mind, and spirit.

My turn-around point came when I received a flier in the mail about a program called "New Directions." It was for single mothers and displaced homemakers. I was a 42-year-old sober alcoholic mother of two elementary school children. The program taught me how to go back to school, and I enrolled as a full-time student in the fall of 1991. I managed to save our home from foreclosure. I managed to rebuild my daycare business. When I was forced to file bankruptcy because of my husband's refusal to pay his debts, I chose to repay my debts instead of discharging them. I believe in self-respect, and I believe in living a life that is responsible and honorable.

I successfully operated a daycare in my home, working sixty hours per week and attending school full-time in the evenings and Saturdays. My educational journey took many years. Scholarships helped me. I remember using some of the money to replace worn brakes and make car repairs on our ten year-old car so that I could attend all my classes. My worn down old car kept breaking down. When that happened, instead of bursting into tears and frightening my young daughters, I would tell them that we were on a new adventure. Then I would call neighbors to tow us home. After too many of these adventures, my daughters told me that they did not want to hurt my feelings, but they would really appreciate it if they did not have to go on any more "adventures" because they were not much fun! I could not agree with them more.

In 1997, I began my first semester in graduate school at Portland State where only 140 students were accepted out of over 800 applicants. I was still working thirty-six hours in daycare and going to an internship for another twenty to twenty-four hours a week. I co-facilitated two women's support groups on domestic violence as well as providing one-on-one counseling. Finally, in June 1999, I completed my master's degree.

Today I have a life that I am proud of. My daughters are strong, healthy women, and both are planning to go to college. I share my story with others every chance I get. I want people to know that there is hope. While it is not always easy, it can be done. There were many nights when I cried on the way to school and I cried on the way home due to exhaustion. We can escape from abusive spouses, and we can rebuild our lives. We can be safe. There is help within the community through people who care. My work is demanding, but I love it. Every time a woman is helped, I feel as if I am striking a blow against dysfunction and disease. I am so grateful for the chance to use my own heartache and pain to help someone else. I am the richest woman I know.

Stephanie I. burns

"Going back to school was like coming back to life! I soaked up every bit. My daughters watched me, and I know it was good for them to see me struggle through my fears and **go after a life outside the traditional lines** as a non-traditional student."

A moment of grace gave me the courage to change careers. I certainly never dreamed that losing my job would lead me to finding my life, but "God often writes straight with crooked lines." In 1989 after a divorce, I became the breadwinner for my family. I had almost no marketable skills, but I took a typing class at the local high school and re-entered the workforce for $5.25 an hour.

Working my way up the ranks, I hit the glass ceiling for a woman with no degree, and I was downsized out of my job. As the shock waves receded, I began to take stock. A career counselor told me I was a classic right brain intuitive creative in a left brain profession. He suggested I look at this as an opportunity to change careers and to think about doing what I loved, rather than looking for work in the field that had unceremoniously spit me out. My work had been in business administration, but my dream had always been to be a writer, and my passion was helping others.

I took a leap of faith and applied for a scholarship to a business seminar for women called, "Exploring Your Business Dream." I wrote a five-year business plan that was the foundation for my dream of a home-based coaching and communications service business.

I never imagined myself going back to school, and the idea of going for my B.A. was intimidating. Although I had been to college in the 1960's, I was not college material then and earned few credits. After I lost my job, I received a Job Training Council Grant for Women in Transition and Dislocated Workers to help me start part-time at the University of New Hampshire.

Taking courses, some thirty years after most people go to school, as a single-parent, a working-mom, and the sole support for my three daughters was very slow going and stressful to the extreme. I decided to apply for scholarships so I could attend full-time, concentrate on my studies, and finish more quickly. I was an English major, and I loved every class. I took fiction writing from a wonderful teacher who had graduated, as I would, in her fifties. She and others like her gave me hope and support; when I once said, "It's too late and I'm too old," she said, "I don't even want to hear you think about giving up — you're right where you are supposed to be!"

My daughters watched me, and I know it was good for them to see me struggle through my fears and go after a life outside the traditional lines as a non-traditional student. I admit I have really always been non-traditional at heart, and I loved being an adult learner in college.

Today, I have reached a number of my goals and discovered a few more along the way. I write poetry and my poems have been published in literary magazines. I also write short stories and plays. I have my own business as a communications coach, and I am the director of a self-publishing company.

For me, going back to school was like coming back to life! I soaked up every bit. What motivated me was the schoolwork — reading, writing, discussing and learning. Now I'm thinking of going back for my master's degree in English education. I want to keep learning, and to pass on what I have learned to others.

"Take it one semester at a time or even one course at a time. **Staying focused on immediate goals helps.** If I had to think about the whole degree and what I was doing, I would have been overwhelmed."

angela mcCrorey

I was truly surprised to hear so much negativity and criticism when I decided to go back to school. I did not expect this reaction from my family and friends. My quest for self-improvement was mine alone.

For many years I had dreamed of earning a Bachelor of Science degree. The first part, earning my associate's degree in science, was a big accomplishment for me. I remember how terrified I was to go back to school. I was working for an hourly wage at a hospital, and colleagues persuaded me to try it saying, "Just for one semester, just see how you can do." I did. A second semester followed the first. Staying focused on one semester at a time or one course at a time helped. If I had to think about the whole degree and what I was doing, I would have been overwhelmed. I didn't let myself worry about long-term goals until my last semester in school.

School broadened my horizons and gave me adult friends. It changed me from being a mother and homebody with a minimum wage job; I grew personally from being with other people who had goals and dreams. It transformed me.

Since graduating in 2002, I have served in several positions as a nutrition specialist. I worked at a hospital where my duties were varied, including individual patient services and administrative tasks. My career headed in a new direction when I took a position with a public school district as director of food and nutrition services. In so doing, I joined the senior staff of the county school district, responsible for managing food service annual budgets and supervising the staff at eight different schools. These tasks are challenging, but I love my work.

In retrospect, going back to school was not something my family and friends supported. They saw me as an older woman who had two sons and a steady job, albeit unskilled labor, paying minimum wage. They thought, "Too old, too late." But, it was the right decision, enabling me to finally have a career that I am proud of.

I have helped my community through my work in our schools and provided financial security for my sons. Even though they loved and supported me, I could not know all of the lessons my children were learning by my example and from my actions. One day, my younger son said something that made my heart melt. He stood among all of the children at his school pageant and waited for his turn to speak. My pride in him turned to surprise when he raised his young, clear voice to announce in front of everyone there, "The most inspiring person for me is my mother." In that moment, it hit me. He did notice all of the effort and determination. I know that when my sons see what I have accomplished, it gives them hope for their own futures as well.

"After a lifetime
of feeling
I didn't deserve
what other people
seem to take
for granted,
I felt I could
hold my head up
and fight
for my right
to a good life.
**Believe that all
your living
has been
worthwhile.**"

Susan frank

My father was killed in a plane crash on
September 14, 1947, and I was born five days later. My
mother and grandmother raised me. I became pregnant at age
fifteen and dropped out of high school. Married at sixteen
and divorced four years later, I went back to high school and
graduated in 1968. Although I started college, I married
again and left after one semester to have my second child.
That marriage ended in 1977. I have always worked in clerical
positions to support my family. I was bound and determined to
buy us a house. It took two-and-a-half years, but I persevered
and we finally moved into our own home.

Instead of completing my own education, I chose to make sure my sons were prepared for life first. Once they were grown, I felt it was my turn. After a lifetime of feeling I didn't deserve what other people seem to take for granted, I felt I could hold my head up and fight for my right to a good life.

To pay my tuition and fees, I used the Veteran's Administration Center remitted tuition vouchers, scholarships, and loans. I paid for the balance myself, putting myself in debt with credit cards. Sometimes my financial situation was discouraging. I had to stop working full time to complete my required field work. That meant surviving on whatever I could earn at a part-time job. If I didn't have tuition money in the fall, the courses I needed to finish up were not offered again until the next fall, putting my graduation off a whole year.

I worked very hard, but needed just enough to get me over the last bit of hard road so that I could graduate. Support from scholarships helped me finish my bachelor's degree as planned. Next, I earned a master's degree in social work as well as my gerontology certificate and the state certification to practice social work.

Helping others, especially the elderly, is how I want to spend my life. Great wealth or material things are not important; I just want the opportunity to earn my living by improving the quality of life for the older people in my community.

I enjoy working in the field of home care as a social worker. When older people become ill or meet with an accident, I help them cope. I am so glad that I'm doing something I can look back on with joy and satisfaction. I am convinced that it's never too late to complete your education. In fact, life experience gives older students an edge over younger students! My advice to older students is: don't feel inadequate or insecure. Believe that all your living has been worthwhile, because it gives the framework for all that you learn in school.

"Do what you really, really like.
If you follow your passions,
you will be rewarded
with happiness."

diane m. bailey

My love of gardening and deep respect for the earth inspired me to return to school. My ambition is to help the environment in every way possible through teaching others to care for our planet and its resources. Gardening is an experience I've enjoyed for my whole life. I have shared it with my grandchildren – on weekends you can find us there digging in the earth. I have studied gardening on my own for twenty-seven years, learning organic and environmentally friendly methods from "how to" books. Eventually my passion led me back to school. My goal was to earn a B.A. in horticulture and own an organic nursery where I could provide workshops for children and adults on sustainable agriculture.

There weren't many financial options for me to attend college when I graduated from high school, so I chose to enter the U.S. Army. Soon after, I met my husband and we started our family together. I put my dreams of a college education on hold and my energy into raising my family. Throughout this time, the hope of someday going to college remained in my mind. Going back to school to finish my education and earn a college degree is the thing I am most proud of. I enrolled in the fall of 2000, working toward a bachelor's degree in horticulture sciences. With the knowledge I taught myself through books and my gardening experience as well as the knowledge I acquired in college, I had the training to forge my own path in the horticulture and landscape business. I waited twenty-five years, earned straight A's, and graduated summa cum laude. In addition to my degree in horticulture, I want to earn a teaching degree. One day, I want to to return to my college to teach part-time in the horticulture department.

One of the unexpected outcomes of my education was discovering that I have a flair for writing. The associate's degree required some broad liberal arts courses including math, art, and English. The English courses brought out the writer I had inside me. When I first opened my nursery business, one of my ideas was to produce a newsletter about plants, plant care, and environmental matters. I hope that this newsletter, along with classes that I give at the nursery to children and adults, will help teach people. I want to share my knowledge along with operating a business.

My advice to other women thinking about going back to school is: Don't be afraid to go for it! Set a goal to do something you really, really love. I've learned that if you follow your passions you will be rewarded with happiness. When I walked across the stage to get my diploma, it was such a thrill! Do it. You've waited long enough!

annette o. longhurst

"Students who go to college later in life **bring something special that both professors and classmates appreciate: maturity and the gift of wisdom.** At the same time, there are wonderful, close friendships to be formed with people the same age as your own children. Their minds are quick, and I often went to them for help."

I have been blessed with many opportunities for growth in my life. I grew up close to an American Indian Resevation, lived in Mexico for eight years as a young mother, and learned to appreciate diversity in people and cultures. The opportunities and challenges associated with raising six children had a strong influence on who I am today. Those experiences, along with spending time with my eleven grandchildren have taught me to appreciate diversity in individuals as well!

In 1966 I attended Brigham Young University on an academic scholarship, but dropped out of school when I married in 1968. For the next twenty-seven years I was a busy full-time mother raising my six children. I volunteered to do music and art history programs in elementary schools in my district and to give music appreciation programs in inner-city summer school programs. I worked as a Head Start teacher's aide with children diagnosed with attention deficit disorder and emotional disturbances. Children with mental and neurological challenges were among the youth served, and I found working with them to be especially rewarding. Music experiences in the classroom brought out the best in these children. Somehow, I knew that music could be a resource for even greater benefit in their lives. I began to dream of returning to school, gaining the tools and training in order to serve. However, I had to postpone pursuing those dreams.

I divorced in 1993 and faced the financial, physical, and emotional challenges that accompany being a single parent. When my mother was diagnosed with Alzheimer's disease, I cared for her for three years. The disease progressed, and she needed twenty-four hour care. I moved to Utah with my father and youngest daughter where my mother could receive care in a facility that offered music therapy. In Utah, I volunteered for the opera company, an adult day care center, and hospice. I became a certified nurse's aide and worked at a rehabilitation center and adult day center until my mother's death. As my father's health declined, I had the opportunity to care for him also. Family experiences with my aging parents, my volunteer work, and my job all combined to deepen my desire to become a music therapist trained to work with the elderly.

The idea of going back to school later in life was daunting. I shared my hesitation with a friend. "But I'll be over fifty when I graduate!" She wisely counseled me, "Yes,

and how old will you be if you don't go back to school?" So,
I enrolled in Utah State University. I quickly found that going
back to school in my later years was much more challenging,
but also much more rewarding than I ever imagined. My life was
very different from what I had pictured as a "cookies and milk"
grandmother.

I graduated Summa Cum Laude with a Bachelor
of Science degree in music therapy and a certificate in
gerontology in 2002. It took an additional year of school
to train for gerontology certification, but the knowledge was
important for my field. Eventually, I came to understand that
I also was serving as a role model for my grandchildren in
helping them value education.

Today, I am employed in my dream job as music
therapist at an adult day center. I am working with individuals
who have a broad range of diagnoses affecting their
physical and mental health. Activities that I provide include
music and movement groups, bell choirs, sing-alongs, and
intergenerational sessions where seniors participate with
children.

Students who go to college later in life bring something
special that both professors and classmates appreciate:
maturity and the gift of wisdom. As an older student, I
discovered how wonderful it is to form close friendships
with fellow students the same age as your own children. It
helped me understand my own children better. My younger
classmates's minds were quick, and I often went to them for
help. In return, they came to me seeking my perspective and
encouragement when the going was tough. It was a special,
deeper sharing. I want other women to believe that if they truly
have a dream, nothing is more rewarding than to make that
dream come true.

"I'm not afraid of storms, for I'm learning to sail my ship."
—Louisa May Alcott

"You gain strength, courage, and confidence by every experience in which you really stop and look fear in the face. . . . You must do the thing you cannot do."
—Eleanor Roosevelt

Overcoming
Obstacles

"You can show everyone, show the world, that they cannot break you. It's important to **show our children how to face up to life's challenges**; show them by our own lives how to keep going how to be strong, and how to persevere. In the end, they will know that whatever comes their way, they can face it."

Carilyn Meenderink

The first paper I ever turned in for English received an F, and the professor thought my skills were so poor that I should drop that class. I was determined and studied everything I could on writing and grammar. The next paper that I turned in got an A. I have managed to earn the respect of every professor I've had since.

I come from a family with no college background and no financial stability. My ex-husband discouraged me from getting my G.E.D. and later discouraged me from going to college. When we divorced, I worked and soon realized that I would never be able to support my family unless I went back to college. As a thirty-seven year old single mother of four daughters, I enrolled in college to study software engineering.

I graduated with a bachelor's degree in computer science/software engineering. The degree did not bring work automatically. I spent three months, night and day, applying for jobs, and worked as hard looking for a job as I did in school. Finally, the perfect job came along, less than ten miles away from home. It is exactly what I trained for! I love every aspect of my job as a software engineer: consulting with my clients on the needs assessments, writing the concepts, developing the software, testing it, maintaining it, and working with the team to improve our products and services.

Now, even after being an employed professional for several years, I am still amazed at the satisfaction I get from writing out and paying all of our bills each month. This is a wonderful feeling. When I look back at my life as a mother of four who supported a family for nine years on welfare, it shows how far I've come. Just standing in line at the grocery store and knowing we can pay for our own groceries makes me thankful for my education.

I remember that during my journey, there were some defining moments, the kind of moments that you can't ever take back. One of these happened when I first decided to go back to school. I thought I was too old. I told my mother, "I'll be forty by the time I graduate!" My mother replied, "You're going to be forty, anyway; so, why not be forty and have a degree?" Another decisive moment was when I finished my A.A. degree. It had been so hard on my daughters to have a mother who was also a student. We had a family council meeting and I asked them if I should continue to go to school for the degree. My daughters gave me the confidence to go on.

Yes, there were many times when I felt like dropping out of school, when the pressures were too much. Even applying for scholarships took a lot of time and effort. But it is worth it in the end. My advice is to keep going. You need to be strong and persevere. You can show everyone, show the world, that they cannot break you.

I see now that my education gave me not only material security: a profession, a livelihood and my first home, but also many intangibles, such as my pride in being the first college graduate in my family and my knowledge that now all my daughters are motivated to continue their education. It's important to show our children how to face up to life's challenges; show them by our own lives how to keep going, how to be strong, and how to persevere. In the end, they will know that whatever comes their way, they can face it.

≡

"My education benefits me because I know that I can do whatever I set my mind to do. The words 'I can't do this' are no longer a part of my vocabulary.

linda Smith-barrett

I began my life in the worst projects you can imagine on the north side of Chicago. I have vivid memories of going to elementary school and seeing people stabbed right on the school steps. I watched an older friend who used to take me and other children to the park get his head blown off. As soon as I graduated from high school, I entered the Navy. I spent fifteen years there, during which time I got married and had two daughters.

I separated from my abusive husband in April of 1991. At that time he vowed that when he got finished with me, I would be living in the projects with my children. He tried to make that threat come true by not paying his share of the bills that we had accumulated together before our separation. He filed for bankruptcy and did not inform me. I learned about this after receiving notice that my home was in foreclosure, and that I had only so many days to get out with my kids in tow. Then, the creditors began to contact me for payments. I eventually had to file for bankruptcy as well.

This situation did not break me; it made me a much stronger woman. I was able to purchase a home for my daughters and me in 1996. Two weeks before my military service ended, I was struck by a vehicle on base and was classified disabled upon retirement. I was laid off from my job as a central billing collector with a car rental firm in November 2001 after the September 11th tragedies and the downturn in the travel industry.

One month later, I was awarded custody of my deceased brother's three sons ages sixteen, fourteen, and twelve. The boys had been living pretty much on their own in the projects in Indiana since their mother went to prison. I learned that my youngest nephew suffers from Attention Deficit Hyperactivity Disorder, something I didn't know anything about. I have since educated myself and have taken steps to help him. All three boys were behind in school. I don't regret that I took in my nephews in spite of people telling me that I was crazy to do so. The oldest of my nephews has obtained his G.E.D. and is serving in the military, while the other two boys, who joined my daughter on the Honor Roll, have returned to their mother in Indiana.

My goal is to work in the juvenile court system, perhaps as a probation officer. I am so encouraged by the fact that I was able to help my nephews turn their lives around that I am all the more inspired to work with troubled children. If I could help my nephews, then, maybe I'll be able to help other kids. Receiving a scholarship from the Jeannette Rankin Foundation enabled me to finish my Associate of Applied Science degree in paralegal, and I graduated on May 2, 2006. I am happy to report that I then received a $25,000 scholarship from Virginia Wesleyan toward my B.A. in criminal justice.

The most important benefit of my going back to school is that it inspired my children; my older daughter is in college and the younger is visiting colleges for the future. They are proud of me. My education benefits me because I know that I can do whatever I set my mind to do. The words "I can't do this" are no longer part of my vocabulary. It has made me a very proud, independent woman, who has beaten the odds in many aspects. You can do anything and everything that you put your mind on doing. Nothing is impossible.

No mountain is too high to climb once you've decided that you want to climb it.

=

"A degree matters to employers because it **shows you can finish what you start**. They admired my commitment to a long-term goal. Today, all four of my children know that going to college isn't an option. The know they'll go!"

Cathy lippert

I believe that all of life is a learning experience, and that education is a tool available to all as long as they live, despite financial obstacles. I am proof of this statement. I never dreamed that I would be an unemployed single parent of four at 36 years old.

27

I thought I was taking the right steps earning my associate's degree in accounting through part-time classes while I owned and operated a business. My company's growth and success took precedence over my education. Now I look back on those years with much ambivalence. While I learned many aspects about business, it was not enough to keep my business from going bankrupt after eleven years of hard work.

Upon re-entering the workplace, I discovered that an *A.A.* degree does not provide adequate income to be financially independent. Instead of turning to social programs for monetary support, I relied on friends and family for help. I had to finish school while working part-time and raising my children. The pressures of returning to school after a prolonged absence were plentiful. My ultimate goal was a Bachelor of Business Administration degree and the pursuit of a good job – one that could use my talents, fulfill my yearning for growth, and compensate me with a good salary.

Making the decision to return to school was the hardest part. At the time, I was a part-time employee and full-time mom. My youngest was eighteen months old. I wasn't so sure about the value of going back to school. Today, all four of my children know that going to college isn't an option. They know they'll go!

Unlike some of the younger students in my classes, I knew what an education meant. I knew that I wasn't going to make a living without a degree. Furthermore, in the future it would be hard to watch other people move up the ladder because they had college degrees and I didn't.

I faced problems with time management, juggling childcare, work and school. My advice is to rely on others for help. That was hard for me to do, yet asking for help led to some great friendships and strengthened bonds with my extended family. Sometimes help came from unexpected sources.

I graduated with high honors with a B.B.A. degree in finance from Davenport University. It was a great feeling – one of extreme satisfaction for accomplishing what seemed to be an insurmountable task.

I work as accountant/comptroller for an agricultural technology firm, the same place where I had worked while going to school. I am happy to be with a company that works around the world with farmers, the people who are feeding the world. Even though my work is basically with figures and accounts, it feels like I'm doing more because I am connected to farmers and the world.

My company acknowledges my education. My salary nearly doubled after I graduated! I am convinced that they gave me the raise not necessarily because of what I had learned in school but rather for my determination. A degree matters to employers because it shows you can finish what you start. They admired my commitment to a long-term goal.

=

"My friends see from my own experience that it's never too late. Now I know I can fulfill my dreams."

Kristee garcia

I am of Hispanic/Native American descent and the proud mother of three children ages nineteen, eleven, and five. The most courageous decision in my life is also one of the saddest. I decided to raise my children with enough knowledge to abstain from the alcohol and drug abuse that plague people of my ethnic background. Unfortunately, in order to fulfill this decision, we are estranged from my children's father. This pains us, but we must do so to prevent further domestic violence, which is also usually part of the cycle of alcoholism. We hope he recovers.

One event that postponed my education for nearly seventeen years was that I was almost killed by a drunk driver on April 15, 1990 in Sacramento, California. I was seven months pregnant with my middle son, and he was born prematurely. Our family had to undergo major changes. Coping with the stress of a critically ill son was overwhelming. Through the grace of God and medical advances, my son has fully recovered. I have devoted one day a month to volunteer for Mothers Against Drunk Drivers to speak to young DUI offenders so they do not make the same mistake and hurt an innocent member of their community.

The greatest hardship that resulted from the DUI accident was that my employer alleged that I was abusing my sick leave, even though I had properly submitted medical documentation. My son was seriously ill. I fought for my rights under the Family Medical Leave Act. My employer denied my rights and I was forced to resign. Soon after, I received a right-to-sue letter against the state for their accusations and their acts against me. Due to lack of money and my having to take care of an ill son, the lawsuit was never filed.

However, this event taught me a very valuable lesson in life. It contributed to my decision to turn this negative situation into a positive one. I chose to pursue an education in the field of human resource management so that I may prevent other families from suffering discrimination based on medical conditions.

I found that pursuing an education was both healthy and therapeutic in my recovery from the tragic events of the past. After finishing my education, I knew that I would be able to support my children by myself. I would be the first Hispanic/ American Indian in my family to graduate from college.

While working part-time and raising a family, I completed my A.A. degree in 2002. Then, I completed my B.S. in organizational management and earned a certificate in human resource management. As soon as I graduated, I became a human resource assistant for a community bank. Then, I became an office manager at DelMonte Fresh Produce, North America, Inc. I am still very motivated to make sure that human resource laws are followed in workplaces. I want to become an advocate for better human resource management, and my next goal is to study for an M.B.A. in executive management.

Now I know I can fulfill my dreams and reach my goals. I've already shown a lot of my friends that it's possible for them to go back to college after years of being away from school. They see from my own experience that it's never too late.

Susan Cothran

"I love working with people and helping them get stronger and healthier and happier. My advice to women contemplating school is to **go for it; you don't know unless you try.**"

I am a divorced mother of two. When my husband walked out, leaving me with two small children, a lot of bills and very little of anything else, I was devastated. I had been employed in the health and fitness industry, and I loved my work. I love working with people and helping them get stronger and healthier and happier. However, after my divorce, I realized that my income had to increase dramatically and I had to choose another path. I needed a career in a field that would not only be personally gratifying but would provide the means to support my children and me comfortably.

My family experiences inspired me to pursue a career in respiratory therapy. My older sister had been diagnosed with acute leukemia, and I was selected to be her bone marrow donor. While she was hospitalized preparing for her transplant, my father suffered his second heart attack and had coronary by-pass surgery. Naturally, we spent a lot of time at the hospital! I became very interested in the various treatments my sister and father underwent in the hospital, and I felt a special connection with the respiratory therapists. Combined with my experience with aerobics and cardiovascular fitness, this career path seemed ideal for me.

I graduated from the Respiratory Therapy Program at Chattahoochee Technical Institute with a 3.8 grade point average. I passed my certification exams and was hired in a full-time position at Egleston Children's Hospital.

When I reflect on the struggle to get that first degree, it's mind-boggling to see what I had to juggle and what corners I had to cut in order to make it at the end of each month. I couldn't believe it when I looked at my first paycheck after graduation and saw that the amount that was being withheld was more than the total of what I had been using as my budget for an entire month! I can't emphasize enough how wonderful it is to have a salary that allows you to pay your bills, to save for special things, and to be independent.

Returning to school let me find out that I did have the capability to finish my courses and reach my goal. I also know from experience that there are people who will help. In fact, ninety-nine percent of the world wants to help you! Financial Aid offices are hotbeds of information; you just have to do a little digging. My advice to women contemplating school is to go for it; you don't know unless you try. On my fridge, a magnet reminds me, "The worst thing is not to fail, but to make no attempt."

"I was told that social work is not a very good paying job. Money is not important to me. Feeling that I have accomplished something in life is. In the end to **empower yourself through education** is the best thing that you can do."

Cheryl Justis

I came from a very dysfunctional family. Verbal abuse was the only type of communication that we received as children. My father was arrested periodically for the violence that he inflicted on us and on the general population that he came across. The only time we could relax in our home and feel safe was when he was in jail.

Growing up. I was told constantly that I was fat. My mother had me on a diet from the time I could remember. Looking back at pictures of myself as a child. I see that I was a perfectly normal weight. not the fat child I thought I was. I understand eating disorders. suicidal ideas. substance abuse. feelings of inadequacy. divorce. single motherhood. I have experienced them all. I have learned that people live with and endure many horrors.

I started in college wanting to be a social worker. When I began working as a records manager/accounting clerk at a drug and alcohol treatment center in the El Paso County Health Department. I knew I had indeed made the right choice. I no longer felt like a misfit because I fit right in with the clients and staff and the loving. warm. environment with unconditional acceptance for who you are. I have been able to serve many diverse groups throughout my work experience. I worked for the state of New Jersey as a residential living specialist for the developmentally disabled. Most of my clients had little or no contact with their families. I understood their feelings.

I also worked in a hospital for the Bureau of Federal Prisons in New Jersey. Again. I saw the need for humans to have a purpose. a goal. and some type of family bond with others. They would explain to me their hopes. family situations. and conflicts. Some of them were very ill: others had socially difficult situations. I could relate to many of the misfits in the prison population. I did not look at them as inmates. but as human beings who had made wrong choices. Again. my experiences of living in an imperfect world helped me talk to and assist people.

I am very proud that I have survived my past and continue to make improvements in my life. I am raising my son by myself without help of any type from extended family members. I was told that social work is not a very good paying job. The money is not important to me: feeling that I have accomplished something in life is. At times, it felt like the work toward earning my degree was taking forever. I just kept going and going. In the end, to empower yourself through education is the best thing that you can do.

$$\equiv$$

"That is what learning is. You suddenly understand something you've understood all your life, but in a new way."
—Doris Lessing

"A woman with a voice is by definition a strong woman. But the search to find that voice can be remarkably difficult."
—Melinda Gates

the power of
education

$$\int z\, dV = \frac{\pi r_1^2}{VH^2}\int_0^h \, \ldots$$

$$\frac{\pi r_1^2}{VH^2}\int_0^h (z^3 - 2z^2 H + zH^2)\, dz$$

$$\frac{\pi r_1^2}{VH^2}\left[\frac{z^4}{4} - \frac{2z^3 H}{3} + \frac{z^2 H^2}{2}\right]_0^h$$

$$= \frac{\pi r_1^2}{VH^2}\left[\frac{z^4}{4} - \frac{2z^3 H}{3} + \frac{H^2}{2h^2}\right].$$

$$\cdots \left[\frac{1}{4} - \frac{2H}{3h} + \frac{H^2}{2h^2}\right]$$

$\cdots$ is $\frac{1}{3}\pi R^2 Z$

The

"My education is not just a choice— **es mi derecho, education is my right;** like the vote, I will exercise it. There is a YOU inside you that doesn't know how to get out, and education provides that release."

magdalena nieves

My story isn't that different from many other fantastic working mothers; what's different is the journey from tragedy to triumph. At forty-three years of age, I have been a married working mother, a single working mother, a battered woman,

41

a battered women's advocate, homeless, and an advocate for the homeless. I've been a Girl Scout mom, a Boy Scout mom, a soccer mom, a foster mom and a grand-mom. The year I returned to school at Pacific Lutheran University I was a sick mom. I underwent radiation therapy for ophthalmic Graves Disease, my quest for knowledge and concerns for my health overlapped.

Much has occupied my time, but nothing unsurviveable, nothing I could not and did not learn from. In the words of Maya Angelou, "When I knew better, I did better."

It was my dream for many years to earn a degree. That dream took twenty-seven years of on-and-off schooling. The hardest thing in school is choosing between maintaining a high GPA or retaining a lot of knowledge. I am not satisfied with walking away with a good grade, though it pains me to fall short in academics. I want my education to permeate my daily life. Doing both is difficult, but it is achievable.

Once graduation was upon me, I pondered the possibilities of a history degree. Three or four of my professors asked me, "Are you going to be an educator?" That made me start to do some self-reflecting on my new goals for the second half of my life. I looked over my life's resume: legislative and state house lobbying, domestic violence surviving, parenting, foster parenting, criminal justice training, child abuse intervening, and more. All of these involved teaching. I realized that I have been teaching all along! And that took me past the fear of "I'm not teaching material." Earning my doctorate in history and indigenous studies will open doors to learn more and to teach at a university level.

I believe that as an educator, you give back more than anyone else in the community. Education is the key to survival, growth, security, and understanding. It opens up all possibilities and takes the bars off of everything. It's not just a gift you give to yourself; it goes back to the people.

Because I am of Puerto Rican and Native American descent, I've spent a lifetime teaching myself, my children, and my grandchildren about our culture, our history, and our language. I have a passion for history, a quest for knowledge and a desire to know the truths of history, the lies and injustices, the truth about what is not studied – and why it's not told.

My current work at a history museum also came full circle. What began as work-study morphed into an internship developing curriculum for museum materials on the Makah Nation. My mentor was a profound role model for me. I could hardly believe it when the director of education asked me to apply for her job. I became the mentor! I began teaching a cultural perspective of history to children from the second to the twelfth grade. The transition from student to teacher came naturally.

I still remember the phone call I received letting me know that I was awarded a scholarship. I had to give the phone to my life partner because I couldn't believe it. It wasn't about the money. It was that there were people out there who didn't even know me but who believed in me and thought I could do it, and they chose me because they thought that I had the potential. That's the dream defined. Women who have come before challenged the obstacles and found a way to re-identify themselves, reclaiming their worth and using their tragedies to feed and create their triumphs.

During the studying, working, and battling my Graves disease, there were times when I thought, "There's no way to do this." But in retrospect, "There's no way I couldn't have done it." The poster of University of California Santa Barbara on my wall is a reminder of which road I choose to go down to continue my work in history, culture, and identity. My education is not just a choice – es mi derecho, it is my right; like the vote, I will exercise it.

I've done a lot in my life, but I am most proud of having raised four incredible, strong, and intelligent Latin American children. My children are proud and determined. They know the value of education and they applaud and support me. I now hope for their educational dreams to take flight.

Education is magical. There is growth and metamorphosis. There is a whole identity in the academic life that goes beyond that of being "mommy" – and by that, I don't mean to demean the importance of that role. There is a YOU inside you that doesn't know how to get out, and education provides that release. Louise L. Hay says it best, "Dentro de ti hay una mujer inteligente, dinamica, capaz, segura de ti misma, viva, alerta y fabulosa. Permitele salir y actuar. El mundo esta esperando / Inside of you is an intelligent, dynamic, capable, secure, alive, alert, and fabulous woman. Allow her to come out and be. The world is waiting."

=

Sandra hengstebeck

"Doors have opened for me. I feel I have a bright future and that **anything is possible.** I am an example to those who may feel unable to make changes in their lives."

When I started attending the university, I had to make a commute of 180 miles round trip because it was the closest college where I could earn my degree. I had finished all my courses at the community college. Although the commute was costly and time-consuming, it was the most feasible way for me. My housing expenses were affordable, and I had a reliable baby-sitter I could trust. My children are so important to me that having a qualified baby-sitter made attending college possible. Since starting school, I never missed a single class.

My lifestyle changed dramatically when I went back to school. As a single parent, I worked part time, attended school full time, and maintained a 4.0 average. My own grades in school and the time I spent with my children have helped them to excel. I never realized that I was capable of doing anything with my life until I started college. The doors have opened for me. I feel I have a bright future and that anything is possible. With my degree I will be able to work in a career that I will find enjoyable and challenging, not just a job.

I still live in the same home where I was ten years ago, but my life has changed in so many ways. I finished my B.A. and completed my master's degree in computer science. Then I had an internship with the U.S. Navy.

Eventually, I began working at the U.S. Marine base. I work as a civilian in the area of telecommunications, supporting computer networks, radio and radar equipment, and programs that are used in the field. Every day I see how my work makes a difference.

Education took me down a whole new road. I can identify two surprising outcomes of my college experience: My son is now in his second year at the university, paying for it all on his own. Because he saw what school did for me, going to school was never a question for him. He was determined to go, and he worked all kinds of jobs to save money for tuition. My daughter, a senior in high school, is looking into college; she, too, has worked unskilled jobs and sees her own potential to do more in her life.

Since going back to school, my attitude has changed— I used to go into everything thinking I would fail, but once I started getting good grades and saw that people had faith in me, I started to feel better about myself. I like sharing my experience and empathy with the high school and college students whom I tutor. I see how they need not only the skills but also the confidence.

I learned that asking for financial aid was a necessity. My Jeannette Rankin Foundation scholarship came at the perfect time. Because the scholarship could be used for living expenses including repairs, I was able to fix the transmission of my car, continue to commute to school, and still live in my long-time home, a great place to raise kids.

The financial support gave me the confidence to continue school. It meant that people deemed me a valuable, intelligent woman capable of achieving my dreams. This conviction gave me the incentive to keep striving and kept me going when things got rough. I didn't want to let anybody down who had had enough faith in me to help me. Today, even I am amazed at what I have been able to achieve.

≡

"I've taught my children to **always help others whenever possible**. You never know when you'll be the one who needs help."

lois Coffia

I began my adult life by working in a factory when I was eighteen years old. I lived the everyday reality of what the lack of education has to offer, and I did not like the results. I always did everything that I could to help people around me, but I realized that I could only help them to a certain point if I did not help myself by furthering my own education.

48

At the age of thirty-eight, I enrolled in college to become a nurse. It was a goal I had dreamed of for a long time. I believe being an "older" college student gave me the determination to get the most from my studies. Because I had already lived through abuse, divorce and poverty, my faith was strong and I knew I could accomplish anything I set out to do. Going to college was one of the best things I'd ever done, but it was financially a rough time. I always took pride in being self-supporting and never expected to need help from anyone, but I found out that I did.

With the help of the first scholarship check from the Jeannette Rankin Foundation, I was able to purchase a home computer. This was vital to my schoolwork as my classes were web-enhanced. I was grateful for the option to apply the award money to areas other than tuition. In fact, the second check helped to repair the transmission in my van. I appreciate that the foundation respects the maturity of its scholars by giving us the choice to use the money in the way that supports us the most while we are working on our education. Without the scholarship, I would have been stressed about how we would overcome these two major financial hardships. Instead, I was able to concentrate on my school work.

I graduated and passed my state certification. I am now a Licensed Practical Nurse, working in private home care with developmentally disabled adults. This is more gratifying than anything I have ever done.

My part-time work permits more time with my family and time to pursue my RN degree, the next step in my education. The support I have received from my husband and children has been crucial. The kids have taken on new responsibilities and learned that if anyone wants to talk to me, they should stand in front of the computer! They respect my "Do Not Disturb, Testing in Progress" signs. And they are all proud of my accomplishments.

Someday I would like to get my degree in psychiatric nursing. My goal is to become a patient advocate for people with mental health issues so that they can receive the help that they desperately need. I hope one day to be a legal advocate for mental health patients and to work as a nurse in a hospital.

Education has given me a different perspective on the world. I value my courses in sociology and psychology. I see, for example, how my elderly, non-English-speaking patients revert back to their native language when they are ill and disoriented. Education helps you see connections that you never knew were out there before. Education makes you reflect and be aware, to see connections between people. Now, when I treat a patient, I see my grandma.

When I was going through rough times, I vowed that I would give back to others one day. Now I have the opportunity to make my promise to myself a reality. I participate in several volunteer programs and I've taught my children to always help others whenever possible. You never know when you'll be the one who needs help.

> "I gained self-esteem and began **making wise choices for my family's future.** At first the goal seems far away, but after a while, time goes by faster."

Sandra Shopteese-Welliver

I am a Native American woman from the Prairie band Potawatomi tribe. My Native American name Pen-Nat-toh-Quah, "Night Flower Woman," was given to me by my grandfather during a naming ceremony. My heritage is an important part of who I am. As a leader in my Native American group for several years, I have held events and organized the annual Inter-tribal Pow Wow held each Memorial Day.

I am also the proud single parent of a fantastic five year old boy. I encourage my son to develop his own interest in his heritage. He participates in a Native American drum group and dances with me at Pow Wows. I make our Native American regalia for these events, and he wears his as proudly as I do. I hope that he will learn from my knowledge and pass on these skills and traditions to his own children someday. As I share my pride in our Native American heritage, I teach him respect for his people and for all people, and expose him to traditions both new and old.

Five years ago I made a choice for my son and myself by leaving his father's home. The relationship was dysfunctional due to verbal, emotional, and alcohol abuse. I wanted more from life for my son and for myself. I gained self-esteem and began making wise choices for my family's future.

Obviously, I am very family-oriented. Recently, my retired parents and adult disabled sister moved into my home with my son and me. We work together for the benefit of all. My parents care for my son while I work and while I am in school. It is comforting for me to know that when I am in evening classes, my son has had a warm meal and is safe in his own bed. My father provides a positive male role model and companionship for my son. Should something happen that my parents are unable to care for my sister, I will become her legal guardian. Living together provides her with a daily routine and familiar setting that helps her feel grounded.

While working full time and being a single parent, I finished my B.B.A. in fewer than four years. I attended intensive classes year round, which meant no summer vacations and no spring breaks. As soon as I completed my degree, I got a promotion at work. I now work for the state in children and family services at a higher rank and salary.

I've pushed others including adult women who need training and job skills to go to school. I've convinced them that they can do it. At first the goal seems far away, but after a while, time goes by faster. Every "A" earned on a report card makes it better. And every report card gets you closer to your goal.

Sandra k. ashley

"I wonder how
many people are isolating
themselves at home,
hiding out,
not accomplishing
their dreams or even
believing they can
no longer dream.
I learned that **others
were strengthened
by my courage,**
and this, in turn,
gave me strength."

I have had ninety percent of my tongue removed because of oral cancer. Muscle was removed from my back and placed in my neck and mouth. I have no salivary glands, no moisture in my nose or mouth and thus, must have constant access to water. Eating is time consuming. I must use my index finger to move the food around in my mouth to achieve chewing and swallowing. Sometimes I had to go without food until after my college classes were finished, fifteen to seventeen hours between meals.

From my own experience, it was extremely difficult to face the public and endure the rejection and humiliation of being different. My first instinct was to isolate myself from everyone, but then I sought counseling. I wonder how many people are isolating themselves at home, hiding out, not accomplishing their dreams or even believing they can no longer dream.

To me, these achievements mean so much more because of having to overcome my handicap. My speech is impaired, and the requirements of college and speaking in front of a group were sometimes exhausting and embarrassing, but I learned that others were strengthened by my courage, and this, in turn, gave me strength.

I chose a career path that would allow me to counsel people who now must live in altered bodies because of accident or illness. I believe I can help people find hope. I believe hope motivates. Without it, most find nothing to live for.

When I graduated in 1997, I was asked by the Class of 1998 to deliver their graduation speech! I am currently working for the State of Michigan for the Department of Human Services, helping people in need with their applications for food stamps, emergency needs, and Medicare. My office is in a hospital, so I have begun to apply my training and personal experience to supporting others. I lead movement workshops for people suffering from health problems, such as Lupus, MS, and cancer. In addition, I have led movement therapy classes as stress relief for my co-workers.

I serve as a support person for a national organization that serves head and neck cancer patients and survivors throughout the country. I've been a volunteer for several years, and I listen to other cancer patients and survivors, offer emotional support, and direct them to additional resources that may help them.

When working with people with altered bodies, I know first hand the journey to finding hope and new possibilities. I discovered my passion for dancing while in school, when I took a required class with a movement therapist. The mind-body connection was personally enriching and powerful. When people are ill, depressed or feel rejected or stuck, movement gets the endorphins going and helps them focus on what they can achieve.

Education was the key to discovering my sense of worth and value. I would like to work on my master's degree in either social work or psychology. Now, I am always happiest when I'm in the classroom.

Cheryl Guardipee

"You will be rewarded with a new sense of meaning in your life, and **your time is filled with purpose.**"

I was born, raised and educated on the Blackfeet Indian Reservation and am a member of the Blackfeet Tribe. As the eldest daughter of nine children, I assisted in the upbringing of my siblings. I am also a single mother of three boys whom I raised by myself and a grandmother of four grandsons, two of whom I am raising.

The population on the Blackfeet Indian Reservation is about 8000 and growing. Very few jobs are available and the good paying jobs require an education. I have worked several jobs in my lifetime, sometimes two or three per day, just to provide for my sons and myself. The wages were little or nothing.

I began my college education at Blackfeet Community College and completed my first two semesters with at 4.0 average and one hundred percent attendance. Going to college has become a large part of my new life. I like how labs are available for people like me who don't have a computer, and how the instructors are part of the community. It is, moreover, a place where my horizons have broadened; the school is open to all people, not just the people on the Blackfeet Indian Reservation.

Receiving the JRF scholarship was important because it gave me peace of mind. I used the money to pay ahead on my rent and utilities. It's good to know that I can study without worrying about the heat in winter and the bills. One way that I show my appreciation for my scholarship is by getting good grades and by planning to use my education to serve my community.

As a parent and grandparent, I see how important an education is. Education should be a priority for our young people. It is vital to their upbringing because it creates and shapes their lives.

I am striving to be a role model both for my children and for other women. If you are struggling with the decision to return to school, I would say this: Yes, it will undoubtedly be challenging, but you will be rewarded with a new sense of meaning in life, and your time will be filled with purpose.

"I personally measure success in terms of the contributions an individual makes to her or his fellow human beings."
—Margaret Mead

"True patriotism is the service of all, to all."
—Helen Keller

giving back

aree baker

"The scholarships
I received
in college were
**a good
investment
in my life,**
in my children's lives,
in the lives of those
for whom I provide
health care,
and in the
community
to which I am
committed
to serve for
the long term."

Years ago, I witnessed a nurse yelling at an elderly patient. Shocked, that day I purposed in my heart to become a nurse and care for the elderly in a proper manner.

It has been a long journey from being an unhappy housewife to being free and earning my first bachelor's degree. Along the way, I've faced many obstacles: leaving my home

country of Thailand, learning a new language, and overcoming
the unhappy environment my husband created for our three
children and me.

As a single parent, it was difficult attending college,
but becoming a nurse was important to me. Fortunately, the
Jeannette Rankin Foundation scholarship eased some of the
strain by allowing me to change from working full time to part
time. As a result, I attribute my success at school to having
more time to study, more time for my children and a more
efficient schedule. Especially as someone studying in a second
language, I needed extra time to write my papers and then get
help proof-reading and revising them.

I worked very hard in school, and am grateful for
the support of those who believed in me. JRF and the other
organizations that helped me on my journey are like the
cheerleaders who hand out water bottles to runners in a race.
I have taken many water bottles along the way, but I finally
reached the finish line and graduated with a Bachelor of
Science in Nursing in 2005. The scholarships I received in
college were a good investment in my life, in my children's
lives, in the lives of those for whom I provide health care, and
in the community to which I am committed to serve for the long
term.

I am presently working as a Registered Nurse at Mary
Greeley Medical Center in Iowa, and I really enjoy my job. I
specialize in medical telemetry and monitor heart problems
in the critical care unit. In the future I would like to get my
master's degree and become a Nurse Practitioner.

Looking back, I see change. For me, education was
not about a job, but about self-esteem and personal growth.
I truly became a different person. I realized that I used to like
being complimented for what I do, for example cooking a
good meal or making the house look nice. Now I know I am
appreciated for who I am. Besides taking the courses for my

program in nursing. I took many other courses and remember that at some point, I realized that the world is huge. It's much bigger than just me and local circumstances. It's so big, you can't see it just from one point of view.

I used to admire so many other people, and it is strange for me to hear my clients say that they admire me now. I also know that my children have been inspired by seeing my hard work as a college student, mom and nurse. It is because I had the opportunity for education and the chance to overcome many challenges in life that I have become an independent person, a good parent, and a productive member of society.

Suzunn rosenberg jackson

"The scholarship
was so much more
than money for school.
It was an
**acknowledgement
that people
believed in me
and wanted
to help me
put my life back
together.**
Your award gave me
back my dignity
and my self-respect."

A bizarre accident at work amputated two of my
fingers, causing permanent nerve damage and partial paralysis
of my left hand. Virtually overnight I became disabled,
unemployable and technologically obsolete. I lost my job of
twenty-six years as a Diagnostic Medical Ultrasonographer. I
was trapped, living in a surrealistic maze of legal complexity
and financial ruin. Suddenly, I didn't belong anywhere.

At 45 years old, living on Medicare and Social Security was unnerving. I needed to find a new way to become a financially independent, contributing member of society. I didn't want to be a prolonged burden on the "system."

Fortunately, as a former Vietnam-era veteran, I discovered that I was eligible for a two-year scholarship under a rehabilitation program for disabled veterans. I began studying at University of Houston in the fall of 1996 for a bachelor's degree.

Imagine! When I returned to school, I had never touched a computer, surfed the Net, nor had I even seen, much less sent, an e-mail. But I tackled that steep learning curve and went on to embrace the computer as a valuable tool. I even chose to focus my studies on computer science and communications, and I served as the coordinator of the Southwest Regional Conference for Computer Programming.

I earned my bachelor's degree in communications in 1999. I did post-graduate studies in chemistry followed by graduate school in environmental management and received seven scholarships. Along the way, I was awarded an internship for the Texas Commission on Environmental Quality in the Galveston Bay Estuary Program, and that turned into a permanent position as Education Outreach Coordinator.

A new and exciting chapter of my story began when I met another disabled veteran, Bill Jackson. He has accomplished more with no legs than every man I've ever met with two whole legs! A retired marine biologist, he is serving his second term as Mayor of Bayou Vista, making me the Honorable First Lady of Bayou Vista. Who would have thought this possible a decade earlier?

Yet I did not come to this happy situation on my own. I owe appreciation to the Jeannette Rankin Foundation, which enabled me to finish my education by giving me a scholarship in my senior year. Much more than the money, it was acknowledgment that complete strangers believed in me and wanted to help me put my life back together. The award gave me back my dignity and my self-respect. Those are values that money alone can't buy. The JRF award is a very powerful gift.

For me, knowing that the foundation was created to honor Jeannette Rankin, a champion for women's rights, is significant. My own grandmother was arrested in the early 1920s for having publicly supported availability of birth control for all women. As her descendent, I want to continue to make changes in the consciousness of humanity.

Another source of personal inspiration is my daughter. I am the parent of a young woman who is independent, remarkably articulate, and mature well beyond her years. I can't take credit for her accomplishments, but I hope I have helped nourish her vibrant sense of self.

Just as I have been supported through challenging times, I too am dedicated to empowering others and serving the community. A few years ago, I donated a scholarship to the Jeannette Rankin Foundation to give back. I know from personal experience that JRF helps women who are trying to make something of their lives. It gives hope to those who need it. Going back to school gave me marketable tools, freedom from welfare, and a new life.

I now want to teach other women what I have learned. My next goal is to write and present motivational speeches to encourage women to pursue their dreams through education. I want to help women take the first step and to believe in what they're doing, even if they're scared. Like Ralph Waldo Emerson said, "Life is not about finding yourself. It is about creating yourself."

"I now know
the purpose
of all the pain
in my life:
it prepared me
to be compassionate
and understanding
in my desire to
help others.
Surround yourself with
people who won't let you quit."

Kathy Wiley

There are no words for the emotional and physical trials that I endured with my son. My son had a difficult time in adolescence. He was violent towards authority figures, and toward me. I spent a great amount of time advocating for services to help him. I had to plea with a judge to place him in a residential facility at age fourteen. He became involved with drugs and spent six months in rehab. After returning home, he was still angry and struggling. I had to obtain an order of protection against him.

Many thought this young man would end up in prison,
but I never gave up on him. I was able to set clear limitations
and expectations. Through many struggles, and with difficult
boundaries, we were able to maintain a loving relationship.

In addition, I have survived many other challenges in
life. I became a mother at the age of sixteen and never finished
high school. I spent many years with an abusive, alcoholic
husband. After leaving this relationship, I raised three children
while receiving assistance from Social Services and working
part time.

I was desperately in need of assistance to complete
my Bachelor of Social Work degree. The public assistance
I received while going to community college was minimal
because they did not feel that I needed to continue my
education. But I knew that I needed a bachelor's degree in
order to obtain employment of sufficient income. Furthermore,
I was determined to continue for a master's degree. The only
hope I had of becoming fully independent was to earn my
degrees.

Education changed my personality. I used to be quiet
and shy, and people would walk all over me. Now I am able to
assert myself and stand up for myself. As I began my college
education, my son began to gain respect for me.

Through my own educational process, my whole world
got bigger; my worldview expanded. I got more adventurous.
I studied things I had never imagined I would be interested
in, such as Russian history. I was inspired by opportunities to
hear Maya Angelou and Coretta Scott King speak. Even now, I
check out what's going on in my community and go to lectures.
There are some wonderful, lasting habits acquired while I was
in school.

I am a life-long learner. I know that education has
transformed me. This sense of adventure and inquisitiveness

was also transmitted to my children. My daughters are more accepting of people who are different from them because they were exposed to that diversity by coming to my classes. My proudest moment was when my son attended my graduation from community college.

I completed my associate's degree in community mental health in 1997 and graduated with honors. Then, I graduated Magna Cum Laude from Marist College in 1999 and began working for Ulster County Department of Social Services as a foster and adoption caseworker. I earned my Master of Social Work from Fordham University in 2003 while continuing to work as a caseworker.

My long-term plan is to be certified for private practice, which means interning for five years and passing the state exam. In the future I'd like to focus my practice on bridging foster parents with birth parents, helping them work together for the good of the child.

I can honestly say to my clients that I know what they are going through. As a high-school dropout and mom at sixteen, I have been there, too. I dropped out of school in ninth grade. I am just as proud of my G.E.D. certificate as I am of my M.S.W., and both of them are up on the wall in my office.

Providing education to my clients is exciting because I love giving people the chance to question and learn. I love seeing people change and love motivating them to move forward out of their comfort zone.

On top of my professional duties in social work, I volunteer in the community. This year I'm inviting my clients to take part in a "Paint the House" campaign in town to help restore some older homes. I want them to know how it feels to give, and to have that positive interaction with others.

I am financially independent. I bought a house for myself and my children with the help of a first homebuyer's club. I am the first person in my family to own a home. These accomplishments prove that given support and opportunity, success is attainable.

My advice is to find positive people and get the negative people out of your life. The best way to reach your goals is to surround yourself with people who won't let you quit. I also thank the Jeanette Rankin Foundation for believing in me, even when I didn't believe in myself. When I got the scholarship, it made me feel that I could do it. I needed that support because there's always a little doubt. I had always been told, "Who are you to do this? Do you really think you'll get anywhere?"

I now know the purpose of all the pain in my life: it prepared me to be compassionate and understanding in my desire to help others facilitate change in their lives. I feel that my life struggles enable me to empathize with others who face challenges in life and to encourage those who feel defeated. I am dedicated to helping families find their strengths and stay together. One of the best things about my work is that I can now empower others. I believe I have an obligation to reach back and help people.

=

hazel gay lee

"I realized that if other people were willing to invest in me, it meant that **they took me and my dream seriously.**"

I am the ninth child of fourteen children. My father only attended 1st grade. My mother finished 4th grade. Since neither of my parents were educated, it took a group effort to support our family. Each of us children worked while attending school. Out of fourteen children, only four of us graduated from high school. After high school, I wanted to attend college but could not afford to do so. I had worked full time during my junior and senior years to help support the family, and my financial support was still needed.

I married and was the breadwinner, earning the main financial support for my husband and myself. His work was very unstable, but he eventually obtained a painting job to help us financially. This was good timing because in that year, after twelve years of marriage, we were surprised with the birth of our first child.

My entire world changed when our daughter was born. From a very young age I had taken care of children, but having my own child was different. I never realized how wonderful motherhood was until I became a mother. It is a great responsibility, but also a great honor. By far, it is the most rewarding, outstanding, and challenging job that I have ever had.

Two years later, our son was born. He was two months early and had all the problems associated with pre-mature births. He required my constant tutoring and involvement in his academic work.

Watching my son struggle to learn, I knew that he needed me to be at home with him. I have always worked, but I took a gamble and quit my job of fourteen years. To survive financially, I opened a day care business in my home. It has been hard work, stressful at times, but very rewarding too.

It was while working with my son and other children that I realized how gifted I was in helping physically and mentally challenged children. Working with children has been the main focus and pleasure of my life these past fifteen years. I have tried to spark a love of learning because I want them to excel far beyond my own accomplishments. I will do anything within my power to see my children, and any other child, achieve their dream.

My experiences finally stimulated me to call the college admissions office. I wanted to help more children, but needed the education to do so. Emotionally, I was willing and ready, but not academically. A degree would prepare me for teaching. I wanted a master's degree in special education so I could help challenged children. It is a commitment and career that I dearly love and was born to do.

I gave up my daycare business and started substitute

teaching; the flexible schedule allowed me to continue working on my B.A. on-line or in evening courses. After I got my scholarship, I sometimes wondered, "Am I really worthy of this?" The award had the impact of making me commit to my goals. I realized that if other people were willing to invest in me, it meant that they took me and my dream seriously. I had felt I owed them success; I had to finish to make good on their investments. I graduated Summa Cum Laude and was the most decorated of graduates, decked out in ribbons associated with awards and achievements.

My first full-time teaching position was with special needs students in the seventh through twelfth grades of a small, rural school. It was challenging, with a long commute and a meager budget. At first I was overwhelmed, but I did my best and had a successful year. The next year, I was hired at a school much closer to my home. I work with middle-school children who have autism.

It was a long journey, but it has paid off. I have a satisfying teaching career now, and my family is much better off. My daughter is a student at UC Irvine. My son shows promise as an artist or designer. I believe that my education gave me independence, not only in financial terms, but also emotionally and spiritually. I am the first person of my family and my husband's family to attend college. This is the reason I am so proud of my high grade point average and my accomplishments.

My advice to others is to prioritize. When a woman goes back to school, there are so many obligations that some things have to go on the back burner. One of my friends once told me to put a note on my refrigerator, listing my top four or five priorities. Then, when there's a time crunch and something's got to give, you can check your list and make sure that you don't jeopardize your top five. There were times when looking at that list helped me stay focused on my education.

"It has taken three and a half decades for me to follow my childhood vision; today I am in a real classroom, and I **love being a teacher.** There are moments when you finally figure it out. I call them 'Aha! moments'. I witness these moments as a teacher with my students in my classroom and they are so rewarding."

michelle high

Teaching is a calling for me; it's more than a career. Years ago as a child growing up, we would play games. I always played school and was the teacher. Everyone else, my siblings and friends, were the students. It has taken three and a half decades for me to follow that childhood vision; today I am in a real classroom, and I love being a teacher.

There are moments when you finally figure out it. I call them Aha! Moments. I witness these moments as a teacher with my students in my classroom and they are so rewarding. My own Aha! Moment happened when I realized I had to commit myself to training to become a teacher. Deep down inside, I knew that teaching was what I was meant to do.

I worked in fashion as an assistant buyer for a clothing company. One day I realized that working in the fashion industry wasn't what I really wanted to do. Sitting behind a desk just was not where I belonged. I had the opportunity to mentor teenage girls through a church program, and that rewarding experience pointed toward my potential to be a teacher. At the time, however, my priorities were having a job and earning an income to provide for my family. It was not my Aha! Moment; not yet.

I was laid off when the company I worked for went out of business and closed down. Thoughts about teaching surfaced again. Everyone tried to talk me out of it. Friends made discouraging comments like, "Teachers don't make much money." When I enrolled in college majoring in education, people told me that my chosen degree program would be too hard.

When I first went to college, I enrolled to study computers. For years I attended night school part time. I was divorced and felt grateful for friends and family who stepped in to help, but I missed spending time with my kids. Although I wasn't excited about my major, I rationalized that computers were supposed to be the future. If I understood computers, I was sure to find a good job that would support my family, or so I reasoned. I was working, taking classes, and caring for my children, my life on track for a practical career that wasn't right for me at all.

One day as I was walking across campus, my Aha! Moment happened. It just hit me. An inner voice proclaimed what I knew all along, "You're supposed to teach. That's where your passion is, educating children." That day, I went down to the college's Education Department and changed my major.

During my student teaching practicum, I taught special needs children. One day the principal came in to observe and was amazed. "You really turned the class around," she said. Kids who were sleeping through class before were now engaged asking and answering questions. The class was eager, attentive, learning – I changed this class, I inspired those kids, and I knew I had really found my calling.

I've learned to stop listening when anyone tells me I can't do something. In the past, I listened to people who said teaching is too hard, and there's not enough money in it. When I finally followed my true wishes toward a career as a teacher, I discovered my ability to connect with children in the classroom. It's the right place for me. It's exciting when my kids come back to me and say, "I did it. I finally figured it out!" It makes me feel like I've accomplished something important for each of them.

I sacrificed because I was determined to teach. It was hard, raising my children, working and going to school. As a single mother, at times I relied so much on friends for support. I felt like I was depending on others to raise my children. Usually the days were very long, combining work, classes, and homework. My kids would come home and we would sit together and study. It helped teach them once they saw me study, too. When they had a test, I'd stop and help them study. One daughter struggled in school, and I showed her how to welcome a challenge. She successfully graduated high school, facing the hard times by telling herself, "If my mother did it, I can do it." Even to this day, she's been helping me study. I realize now, that my example of going to college later in life taught my children so much about following their own dreams and the value of an education.

≡

barbara robinson dixon

"It's amazing how a small scholarship can make such a huge difference down the road. It helped me get started, and it was the beginning of much larger things."

It happened out of the blue. In response to a call for volunteers in my local newspaper, I sent an email. "I was the first recipient of the Jeannette Rankin award and I would be honored to volunteer my services. My former name was Barbara L. Robinson." In that moment, more than a quarter of a century in time elapsed, allowing the past and the present to come full circle. My story describes the years between.

I ran away and got married at sixteen, had children, worked part-time, and put my heart into raising my family. My husband became ill with cancer. During his last months, weeks, and days, he received special care in the hospital. I literally lived there for seventy-seven days. Ten months after he fell ill, he passed away. I became a widow with two daughters.

I knew I had to support our daughters, but I also knew that I wanted more than just a paycheck and a job. I wanted to become a nurse. I felt I had to do it. I just had to. But how? My friend is a nurse who stayed with me in the hospital during that terrible time. She pushed me to go to nursing school. She kept saying, "You can do it!"

I was lucky to have so many people on my side. I started at our local technical college, and they gave me some financial support. Some of my instructors put their confidence in me. One day, an instructor told me, "There's a new scholarship available. You'd be perfect for it!" They were speaking of the recently chartered Jeannette Rankin Foundation's award to help women over age thirty-five go back to school.

I applied for it, writing about my situation and my desires for the future. Eventually, I heard that I had been selected for the award. The scholarship was great! We needed the money. But even more valuable was the confidence I received from the women who were the founders of the Jeannette Rankin Foundation. It's amazing how a small scholarship can make such a huge difference down the road. It helped me get started and was the beginning of much larger things. With my degree in nursing and new career, I was able to send my daughters to college.

My daughters supported me in pursuing my goal, though at times I truly wondered, "Will this really work?" One daughter was a college freshman when I went back to school; she's a nurse now. My other daughter was a junior in high school; she earned a degree in radiology. Funny, at one time, all three of us worked at the same hospital in Athens!

My education gave me the training I needed for a wonderful career. I learned so much, and I enjoyed it. In nursing, you have some very sad times, but also some very happy times. Both in the area of dialysis where I worked for twelve years, and in home health care, which I have been doing for the past fourteen-plus years, I developed some very close relationships. Sometimes I get very close to some of my patients and their families.

I definitely changed as a result of education. By going back to school I became an independent person. I chose a profession that required giving of myself, and I learned that, indeed, I had it inside me to do that.

Many years later, after I had remarried, and after I moved back to the Athens area, I saw a notice in the paper about the Jeannette Rankin Foundation. The announcement called for volunteers. I responded, and I'll never forget the excitement of that moment of re-connecting. It is wonderful to have a chance to come full circle. It's almost a miracle, but I believe that some things are meant to be; we are on the path that we're meant to go down.

For anyone who is contemplating school or returning for a degree, all I have to say is you have to go for it. The reward you'll receive will far outweigh any fear.

I'm so glad to be able to participate in celebrating the founders, the foundation, and all of the women who have gone back to school. I am proud to be giving back to our community through my work as a nurse. I'm also proud to contribute my time as a volunteer for the Jeannette Rankin Foundation. It has been three decades since I became the first scholarship recipient, and I want to help other women succeed through education.

═

"The education and empowerment of women throughout the world cannot fail to result in a more caring, tolerant, just, and peaceful life for all."
—Aung San Suu Kyi,
Nobel Peace Prize Laureate

"We must not, in trying to think about how we can make a big difference, ignore the small daily difference we can make which, over time, add up to big differences that we often cannot foresee."
—Marian Wright Edelman

Changing Myself and My World

marsha m. peterson

"I learned what it means to be part of a community, and what building community means; **I learned about people; in doing so, I learned much about myself.** It is my hope that the transformative change in our family will continue to impact their futures and benefit the world in which my grandchildren and their grandchildren will live."

When I applied for the Jeannette Rankin Foundation scholarship, I had completed over five hundred hours on building sites for Habitat for Humanity. In each of those hours, I learned something. I learned what it means to be part of a community, and what building community means. I learned practical things about drainage, construction, insulation and roofing, but more interestingly, I learned about people; in doing so, I learned much about myself.

My goals are to help "the man farthest down," working for justice and to make a difference in the world. The compassionate and caring Dr. George Washington Carver stated, "Without justice, there can be no peace." In a further call to action Dr. Carver states, "no individual has any right to come into this world and go out of it without leaving behind him a distinct and legitimate reason for having passed through it." At age thirty-eight, I knew that in order to find my distinct and legitimate reason, I would need an education.

In school, I specialized in accounting for nonprofit and governmental applications. This training in accounting and public administration is essential to my work. Without the skills attained through my education, I would not be able to serve others – because it takes a lot more than good intentions to solve problems.

I am also the mother of six children. They are my first reason for living the life of service and dedication to peace and justice. I am their example. They have spent hours helping me with Habitat and other community service projects. Because of my hard work and dedication to my education and service to my community, they appreciate their own education and are aware of social justice issues. Ultimately, it is my hope that each of my children will follow me through the doors of higher education and into the world of service, either in their small corner of the world or beyond. If I can see this in my lifetime, I know that I will have left behind "distinct and legitimate reasons for having passed through" the world.

Upon my graduation with my Master of Public Administration degree, I served as the CEO of Habitat for Humanity for Iowa. I oversaw thirty-six affiliate offices throughout the state and much of my work included project

management, budget allocation, and administration. I
liked helping to solve problems so that more families could
have affordable, safe homes and fulfill their dream of home
ownership. In 2007, I took a new position with the budget and
finance division in the Iowa Department of Natural Resources.
Through my work, I help people to implement policies. This is
another form of public service, and it is rewarding. I am using
my business and accounting training while working together
with people to build better communities for today and future
generations.

I appreciate the Jeannette Rankin Foundation
scholarship because it told me that my goals are important,
that I could attain them, and that I would contribute to society.
Especially for people who have been devalued in the past, there
is a huge value in having people who don't even know you tell
you that you are valued.

In my life, I can see the impact that my scholarship,
college education and professional career made on my
children. My children range in age from the oldest, who is
twenty-three, to the youngest, who is ten. When I was in
college, my example gave a message that higher education is
critical. The outcome is most evident today in my youngest
child. There has never been an ounce of doubt in my youngest
daughter's mind about college – she is going. She has career
goals, and I think that she will go on for an advanced degree.

Through my own eyes, I can see the generational
change in outlook and expectations. It is my hope that the
transformative change in our family will continue to impact
their futures and benefit the world in which my grandchildren
and their grandchildren will live.

Sandi Pierce

"Choose friends carefully.
Cultivate people on the
same path of high goals,
and choose people
who will support you
and the history of
who you are,
not those who will
criticize or create doubt."

I'm smart. I'm capable. And I'm deadly serious about getting an education. I've spent a lifetime working at jobs that had no future, ignoring my own dreams in order to pay the bills.

I own every label that can be applied to disadvantaged women. I'm a survivor of six generations of incest and alcoholism, the first in my family to seek recovery. I was a battered wife for thirteen years and have been homeless, disabled, and jobless. Eleven years ago, I started therapy, sought help and began to rebuild.

I was a forty-three year old single mother raising a six year old boy. I was a commercial baker for nine years. I suffered a permanent lower back injury that made it impossible to do the heavy lifting necessary to my career as a commercial baker. As a result of my injury, I lost my job. My son and I were forced to go on welfare, and I was referred to vocational rehabilitation. I needed a college education to lift us out of poverty.

Though I received no income, vocational rehabilitation paid my tuition for two certificates in Drug and Alcohol Counseling at the University of California Santa Cruz Extension. I was the first person ever to be sent on to the Advanced Certificate by vocational rehabilitation, and when I was halfway through the program, my counselor chose to put my case on hold, encouraging me to go to college and get a degree. During my first semester at Cabrillo College, I went to school seven days a week.

I begged my friends to baby-sit on weekends. I completed the certificate program and finished the semester at Cabrillo with straight A's. As part of the program, I also completed a five hundred-hour internship in a chemical dependency treatment center and an honors independent study program in psychology.

It was a terrible time, but I didn't quit and I didn't lose sight of my goals. And I did reach those goals. I have a B.A. in sociology, an M.A. in sociology, and a Ph.D. in sociology. I now work as a research scientist, conducting practical, applied research in social service projects directly taking place in the community.

Receiving the Jeannette Rankin Foundation scholarship was very empowering. I got no affirmation as a child, no feedback on my abilities or skills. I made poor life choices in order to get affirmation, to be liked. Receiving the award was also very healing. Instead of getting pity, it was as if the JRF scholarship gave extra acknowledgment to women for their agonizing, painful histories. I learned that what I had was experience, not shame.

I was ashamed when I was a victim of my husband's rage, but today our lives have turned around. It has been a long road of treatment and recovery. The perspective of my native culture taught that talking about myself was bragging. In school, I learned how to believe in myself and to talk about myself in a positive way. College taught me that hard work is rewarding and brings affirmation. My advice to women re-entering school is to choose friends carefully. Cultivate people on the same path of high goals, and choose people who will support you and the history of who you are, not those who will criticize or create doubt. Build friendships, work hard, and finish school — because the whole point is to get through and then go on to do work that makes a difference!

=

ardella hudson

"I am the product of social welfare. It was **a challenge that I had to face whether I wanted it or not.** I belong to four generations of the struggles of African American women to free themselves from welfare and poverty. Never forget or underestimate the greater power within yourself."

Six year ago. I was shot in the head at close range. The bullet went into my frontal lobe. I went through rehabilitation at the Sister Kinny institute for Traumatic Brain Injury.

I am a 48 year old African American woman. I am the product of social welfare. It was a challenge that I had to face whether I wanted it or not. I belong to four generations of the struggles of African American women to free themselves from welfare and poverty.

I was a heavy equipment operator for twenty-one years. I raised one child as a single parent. He is now thirty-one years old, and his career centers on computer technology. I am also the primary caregiver for my sixty-nine year-old mother.

It is a radical change to go from social welfare to the Dean's list at the College of St. Catherine. The style of teaching and the elements I am being exposed to at the College of St. Catherine, a private college for women, has allowed me to gain self-knowledge, and I am able to be honest about who I am and what I feel. I have stick-to-itiveness, and I am determined to graduate so that I can better serve the needy of St. Paul and Minneapolis. I have a deep commitment to provide competent and professional services to people who need them. I am dedicated to helping others in a non-judgmental and patient way, including the homeless, people of color, gay and lesbian people, chemically-dependent people, the aging population, and people who have been exposed to violence.

I believe in social justice for all.

I have been on a personal growth journey as a student that has opened me up to many new possibilities. After earning my B.S., my next goal is to earn my Master of Social Work with a special focus on law and public policy.

I see a great and increasing need for advocates in government, especially as budget cuts and legislation affect the poor and the homeless in ways that minimize their representation and support. Services to individuals and community agencies have been cut in recent years. I see the struggle and the opportunities to make change, and so I volunteer with the Minnesota House of Representatives.

I have received several awards, such as the Abigail Quigley McCarthy Award for social justice and leadership and a scholarship from the Minneapolis Women's Rotary. Of all the recognitions, I still recall how overwhelmed and honored I was by the Jeannette Rankin Foundation scholarship – because of what Jeannette Rankin stood for as a pioneer. I can't emphasize enough how all awards have a deeper meaning beyond their cash value. The financial support is important, but even more lasting is the sense of affirmation and moral support.

Never forget or underestimate the greater power within yourself. Strengthened by my faith, I found education to be my turning point. Education not only benefits the individual as an intellectual vehicle to success, but it also is an added benefit to society when one chooses to give back to the community from which one came. I want to use my education to help my community grow.

I urge women to go back to school. I'd say to anyone who is contemplating it, even if they have been out of school for years, "It is never too late. You are worth it."

"No one tells you how to do it. You stumble and get no sleep. But you **love it and you never want to let it go.** My education made such a difference in my life."

Iynda Kenney

I remember being at the reference desk of the University of North Dakota library and finding out about how the Jeannette Rankin Foundation scholarship was for women my age who were living on a low income. I felt it was calling out to me. I was desperate and that was the first scholarship I ever received. Being selected for the JRF scholarship in 1986 was like winning the lotto!

Even with the foundation's help, I still needed to take out more loans. My daughters, who are now grown, refer to the days when we lived in campus family housing with a certain fondness as "when we were poor." Even though I am still paying back my student loans, I'll never complain about writing checks for my education repayment – because my education made such a difference in my life.

I earned my B.A. in journalism from the University of North Dakota in 1992 and was encouraged by my professors to continue on with graduate work. I did, and earned an M.A. in communication in 1996. During my graduate studies, I worked as a graduate teaching assistant and taught several courses independent of a professor. It was so rewarding that I realized that I wanted to continue teaching at the college level. I earned a Doctor of Education degree in Higher Education/Teaching and Learning in 2002.

After teaching for a decade, I became been an Assistant Professor in the Department of Technology. I am the only female professor in a department where ninety percent of the students are men and ten percent are women. I direct a new major, Graphic Design Technology, teaching graphic communications, web design, print graphics and animation. I've been nominated for a number of teaching awards locally and nationally. Of course, I'm happy to be honored – but it's like frosting on the cake to get awards for doing what you love to do!

I am the first in my family to be a college graduate. It wasn't that I was prohibited or discouraged from going to college; it was simply that nobody talked about it or had any expectations. My parents noticed a change in me and encouraged me to continue with my education. They told me that my ideas, the way I think and how I listened to people grew broader and had more depth. I think that for me, re-entry to school was like having your first child. No one tells you how to do it. You stumble and get no sleep. But you love it and you never want to let it go.

=

"My advice for women who are returning to school is to start slow, take one class at a time and build a supportive network. What builds self esteem in a child is mastery of skills; **skills can be taught, practiced and mastered through education.**"

april moore

W hen I was in high school I didn't think I was smart. I took school for granted. In college, I discovered that I really am smart, and I realize now that I was smart in high school too – I just didn't see it.

I am 39 years young and a survivor. In my years I have experienced sexual abuse, family illness, divorce and poverty. But I don't call any of my life adventures mistakes, because through challenges I found the strength to take a risk, quit my job, relocate and return to college. I finally pursued my lifelong dream and earned my teaching degree. I wish I could have appreciated my academic ability when I was younger. As a teacher I can help young girls and boys to see their potential and strive for their own dreams.

I have three children, all boys. Being a single mother and a college student at the same time was difficult. You learn how to juggle and you don't sweat the small stuff! I gained strength knowing I was setting a good example for my children. I couldn't have a full-time job, take classes and care for my children all at once, and our family struggled financially to make ends meet. One year, times were so tough we wouldn't have had Christmas without help from my parents. But I knew that college education was a good investment in my family's future, and there were other kinds of rewards along the way.

I told my kids the truth about what we had and what we could be appreciative of, and they supported me. While I was in class, my sons pitched in and helped take care of their younger brother. We studied together at the kitchen table. Helping each other, working together, our family became closer. I brought my kids to all the service projects that I participated in, including beach cleanups, volunteering for the deaf and blind and more. Service gave my children opportunities for leadership and it was gratifying to help others. I am teaching my kids that they belong to a community.

Recently, I went to a seminar where I had lunch with a group of women. The woman sitting next to me told me she tried to go back to college but quit because it was too hard. My advice for her and other women who are returning to school is to start slow, take one class at a time, and build a

supportive network. The key is getting a good mentor. Network
with people who have been in school longer. They will be
supportive because they're already in school. Your friends
and family might not be supportive because they never went
to college themselves. Learn as much as you can about your
program and other opportunities to be involved. Ask a lot of
questions so you have an accurate picture of what's going on.
Feel like you're in charge of your own course.

I graduated in 2007 with a B.A. in science and
chemistry. Today I am working as a program manager at
the University of North Florida Environmental Center where
I gained experience working as a student. In my position, I
coordinate environmental study projects on the St. John's
River. I work with college students, and I also mentor chemistry
students. At times I feel like part mentor and part mother hen,
because I am old enough to be their mother!

Female science educators can have a tremendous
impact on their students. I had two incredible mentors in
college, and if not for their wisdom and support I would not
have taken the classes that led me to the job I have today. My
hope is to be a mentor to help girls and young women see their
potential and strive for high goals as future scientists. What
builds self esteem in a child is mastery of skills; skills can be
taught, practiced and mastered through education. Students
should not limit themselves by thinking they are not smart
like I did as a girl. Through mentoring and encouragement,
students can envision themselves as high achievers, college
graduates, and leaders at their workplaces. That is my goal: to
build a brighter future through my experiences and mentoring
the next generations of rising students.

Suzette l. dotson

"Stick with your decision and follow through to your goal no matter how traumatic your past has been and no matter what obstacles you face now. Never settle for less than you can do."

T he poet Muriel Rukeyser wrote, "However confused the scene of our life appears, however torn we may be who now do face that scene, it can be faced and we can go on to be whole." Indeed, my journey to "go on and be whole" has been intense, exhilarating, and exceeds even my wildest dreams.

In April 1996, I made a conscious decision to rise above the personal adversities associated with domestic violence, victimization, and chemical dependency. That moment of clarity was my first step on the road to renewed self-respect, self-improvement, and personal development. With the assistance of a progressive community and dedicated academic counselors, this road led me to Santa Rosa Junior College, and to Sonoma State University. I've earned a B.A. in sociology, a B.A. in American multicultural studies, and an M.A. in counseling, marriage and family therapy. As a family support counselor, I am able to provide support and funding resources for homeless and at-risk families.

For many years, adversity, victimization, and self-destructive behavior obscured my potential and my capabilities. Seeking higher education and entering the world of academia was very rewarding in many ways. My experience in college was an awakening. I earned several recognitions, winning a number of awards and making the Dean's list at both Santa Rosa Junior College and at Sonoma State University. Each acknowledgment enriched and intensified my aspirations to excel personally, academically, and professionally.

Academic achievements, work experiences, and extracurricular activities interconnect as well as overlap. One would not work well without the others. Together, they enable me to pursue my career objectives with conviction, fervor, and persistence. My faith, hard work and determination to succeed will not allow me to surrender each time I encounter an obstacle. Eleanor Roosevelt once said, "You gain strength, courage, and confidence by every experience in which you really stop to look fear in the face. . . You must do the thing you think you cannot do." I believe that says it all.

When I reflect on what I have gained through my education, the most important outcome is that I developed a sense of self-esteem and personal value. I began with the modest goal of getting a certificate from junior college, but was prodded further when my daughter repeated my own advice to never settle for less than you can do.

I advise other re-entry students to stay determined. One professor responded to my doubts by telling me to fake it until I made it. By facing my fears, I found out that I could do it. When that little voice inside you starts to doubt and say, "You can't do it," just remember that maturity is the ability to make a decision and stand by it. Stick with your decision and follow through to your goal no matter how traumatic your past has been and no matter what obstacles you face now.

"We are defined by the way we treat ourselves, and the way we treat other people."
—Oprah Winfrey

"I believe women have something special to contribute to the progress of civilization: the belief in the power of a sustained passion for the ideal."
—Jeanette Rankin

Supporting
the dream

jeannette Pickering Rankin

"What one decides to do in crisis depends on one's philosophy of life, and that philosophy cannot be changed by an incident. If one hasn't any philosophy in crises, others make the decision."

June 11, 1880 – May 18, 1973

Suffragist leader, first woman in Congress, life-long pacifist, advocate for a more open and direct democracy, Jeannette Rankin became and remains an inspiration for upward-bound women. Rankin is remembered in the public mind most often for her anguished votes against United States entry into World War I and World War II. Nevertheless, Rankin's legacy transcends her courageous stands of 1917 and 1941.

Trained as a social worker, Rankin's early work in settlement houses and orphanages convinced her that the solutions to human problems— particularly those of the poor – lay in the political arena. The needs of women and children in poverty would only be met when women held the power of the ballot; so Rankin devoted her efforts to the Women's Suffrage Movement. In addition to extensive nationwide involvement, she led the successful drive for women's voting rights in her home state of Montana in 1913 and 1914.

Jeannette Rankin's 1916 campaign for the United States House of Representatives stressed the need for a woman's viewpoint in Washington. Her viewpoint proved to be compelling to Montana voters and Rankin was sent to Congress on a high progressive platform for social and political reform. Her platform included: pledges to work for national woman suffrage, child welfare legislation, tariff revisions, prohibition, education issues, an absentee voter law, a corrupt practices act, direct popular election of the President, the "one man – one vote" principle, and greater publicity of the activities of Congressional committees. She kept her promise to work for these issues and a number of the bills Rankin introduced broke ground for measures adopted in subsequent decades.

As an activist for peace, Jeannette Rankin was first called to vote her conscience against United States entry into World War I. The House vote was 373 ayes to fifty nays. Rankin's was perhaps the most controversial of the votes against the war. Because of her prominent role in the Women's Suffrage Movement, Rankin was heavily lobbied by other suffragists who felt that if she voted against the war, such an action would hinder the suffrage movement's chances. But the heroic pacifist always took pride in the fact that the first expression of a woman in Congress was against violence as a tool to resolve conflict. From that April day in 1917 until the end of her life in 1973, Jeannette Rankin kept on saying "NO" to war.

Rankin's district in Montana was gerrymandered away and she lost a 1918 bid for the Senate. Returning to "private" life, she continued to work for social legislation, especially through the National Consumers' League. In 1925, she purchased a farm near Athens, Georgia, to serve as her east coast home base. She soon became an activist in the Women's International League for Peace and Freedom, helped to organize the Georgia Peace Society, and became a field representative of the Women's Peace Union. From 1929 to 1939, Rankin served as a lobbyist for the National Council for Prevention of War.

Watching the pressures again build toward war, Jeannette Rankin decided to run for a second term to Congress in 1940. She was elected on a pacifist platform and determined not to seek reelection to public office if the United States declared war during her term. Following the Japanese attack at Pearl Harbor, Congress did declare war, and Rankin once again found herself

in a minority. This time, hers was the only vote against United States entry into World War II. Though vilified and ridiculed, she never regretted her vote. John F. Kennedy said of her in a 1958 article, "Few members of Congress have ever stood more alone while being true to a higher honor and loyalty."

In keeping with her prior conviction (and no doubt political reality), Miss Rankin did not again seek public office. During the 1940s and 1950s she devoted herself to the care of her elderly mother, private study and correspondence, writing and travel. She spent time in Georgia and Montana as well as abroad.

The Vietnam War brought Jeannette Rankin back into the public arena to speak once again against war. "The Grand Old Lady" of the Peace Movement took her anti-war message to podiums all over the country. On January 15, 1968, several thousand women joined the "Jeannette Rankin Brigade" to dramatize their war protests in the nation's capital.

True to form, Miss Rankin used this revitalized publicity to call attention to her collateral concerns for other political and social reforms. Her proposal for direct election of the President, preferential voting methods, and her fifty-year commitment for "sunshine legislation" found a new generation of proponents. A sage observer as well as a participant in nine decades of feminism, Jeannette Rankin commented in 1970 on the "new" women's movement: ". . . men are not the enemy.

It is a woman's responsibility to free herself, and she has not accepted that responsibility."

Jeannette Rankin died quietly in her apartment in Carmel, California, at the age of ninety-two. She bequeathed a part of her estate in Watkinsville, Georgia, to be used to assist "mature women workers" in their quest for independence. Her long-held dream of developing the famed "Round House" as a self-sufficient home and communal center for women did not materialized during her lifetime. However, through her bequest, she has made it possible for the Jeannette Rankin Foundation to carry on this dream. The foundation serves as a living memorial to the great woman whose courage and vision continues to inspire us as individuals and as a nation.

Gail Dendy
Jeannette Rankin Foundation Founder

the jeannette rankin foundation

"What wonderful
work the Jeannette
Rankin Foundation does."
            —Rosalynn Carter

The Jeannette Rankin Foundation is unique in the United States as a non-profit organization dedicated to raising funds for and awarding scholarships to low-income women, ages thirty-five and older. Each scholarship recipient has a vision of how a college education will benefit herself, her family, and her community. Most recipients are in truly meager financial circumstances and may have other hardships or disabilities.

The foundation honors the name and legacy of an American woman of incredible spirit and determination by providing much needed aid to women with the same attributes.

Rankin bequethed a portion of her Georgia estate

to assist "mature, unemployed women workers." Rankin's personal assistant, Reita Rivers, along with friends Sue Bailey, Gail Dendy, Margaret Holt, and Heather Kleiner, decided to establish a foundation to help adult women who face difficulties when returning to school.

The $16,000 in proceeds from the sale of Rankin's property was the seed money for the Jeannette Rankin Foundation, which has been helping mature, low-income women since it was chartered in 1976. In 1978, JRF awarded one scholarship in the amount of $500. In 2008, JRF awarded eighty scholarships in the amount of $2,000 each to women all across the United States, and continues working toward its mission to help women succeed through education.

Jeanette Rankin Foundation
- A Pictoral History

First Scholarship Awarded, $500
to Barbara Dixon, 1978

July 9, 1976
Charter and Articles
of Incorporation

First Annual
Meeting,
Georgia
Center for
Continuing
Education,
1978

Rankin's
Shady Grove
property sold
for $16,000,
1978

Scholarship
raised to
$1500
25 Awards
1998

Spelman
College
Tea Event,
1997

20 Awards
1996

Scholarship
raised to
$2000
30 Awards
2002

Winners of Hat Contest,
High Hat Tea, 2004

Annual
ng, held
nkin's
ated
d House,

First
Board
Retreat,
Sapelo
Island,
1981

JRF Logo is
designed by
Greta Kleiner,
1986

Scholarship
raised to
$750
5 Awards
1983

Jeannette Rankin Day Proclamation
Issued by State of Georgia, June 11, 1980

Epting Tea, 1994

10 Awards
1990

Scholarship
raised to
$1000
4 Awards
1986

Purchase of Office, and
80 Scholarships
Awarded, 2008

n the House"
ersary, 1996

30th Anniversary
Celebration
78 Scholarships
Awarded, 2006

Annual Dinner at the Classic
Center, 2005

Milestone: $1 Million total
in Scholarships Awarded, 2007

111

why give?

Why write this book? The question is one that I have asked myself many times. With each introspection, the answer returned to the core idea: these stories need to be told.

When we allow ourselves to dream, our imaginations wander, taking us to unexpected places. "It is my dream job, and I love it," writes one woman in this book. That is how I felt when I began working at Jeannette Rankin Foundation. Imagine – an organization that gives scholarships to help women who otherwise wouldn't be able to go to college – empowering them to reach their goals. How rewarding! When I started at the foundation, one of my first dreams seemed far away: create a book that would tell the stories of women succeeding through education.

Within months, I met Tom Payton, who rekindled the idea of a book. Soon after, Suzi Wong expressed her passion for the project and offered to take on the interviewing and writing process. Just like the years it takes our scholarship recipients to complete their coursework, so too this book has taken time to come to fruition. As the final words complete this manuscript, I hope that these stories will serve to thank everyone who started this scholarship program and who carry out the work today. Further, I hope that some readers may be inspired to support the foundation. The following section includes the words of a few people who tell their own answers to the question, "Why give?"

—Sue Lawrence
Executive Director

113

I recall when our small group had only around one hundred scholarship applications to go through. It was in the early 1980s, and we all worked together to read and select the scholarship recipients. I continue to volunteer my time with the application review and selection process—and it is still challenging to determine which women among the hundreds who need it will receive the Jeannette Rankin Foundation scholarships.

The reason that the foundation's work appeals to me is because it focuses on women who are going back to school later in life, as adults. In 1981, I started back to graduate school at the age of 58. It was very energizing for me and engaged my mind and spirit in new ways. It helped me embrace the idea of helping women who had been abused, single mothers with children to care for, and women with other difficult backgrounds—helping them to get their education, to become independent and to be in charge of their lives!

I knew people in the community involved with the foundation and the founders. At our core, we knew that education was most important to help people who wanted to move their lives in a new direction. My husband Michael was a volunteer for years also, and we both enjoyed being part of the organization together. Seeing women emerge with a new sense of direction and achieve success is inspiring.

I support the foundation because I can see the results of education – how it affected me personally and how it helps other women achieve success. When Michael died, it was appropriate and fitting to honor his memory by endowing a scholarship through JRF, where we shared in supporting the program. The foundation's work will continue in years to come, helping many more women embark into new lives. My husband's name will live on through the women and families who are helped along the way with the Michael Erlanger Award.

—Mary Erlanger

My paternal grandmother had been a sharecropper, working in a jeans factory when she married at sixteen. By nineteen, my grandfather left her and she was divorced with two children. Despite being a single parent, she managed to provide my uncle and father with a good home through very meager means. Living through the depression had given her a frugal mindset.

Listening over the years to her stories about growing up, I have always been inspired by her. She lives in such a way that there seems to be no obstacle too big to overcome in order to have a fulfilling, happy life. No struggles are too harsh to overcome. This incredible determination toward goals seems to be part of all Jeannette Rankin Foundation scholars. Their lives aren't always easy, but they push through the hard times in order to make a better life for themselves and their families.

My grandmother didn't have the opportunity to go to school, but a college education was so important for her children and grandchildren. We all have benefited from her tenacious spirit, and we also have used our educations to build better lives in our families and our communities. The Jeannette Rankin Foundation helps women who are living in poverty—women who are tenacious like my grandmother — and that is so valuable to them to overcome poverty. The JRF scholarships are so effective for the scores of women who need a little bit of help to go to college. I want to do my part to help more women, and that is why I volunteer my time and contribute to the foundation.

—Juniper Burrows

By serendipity, I bumped into Reita Rivers, who is a Jeannette Rankin Foundation founder, and who served as Rankin's personal secretary. As a history teacher from Newnan County, Georgia, I knew all about Jeannette Rankin, and my chance meeting led to friendship with Reita. I was inspired by the foundation formed to honor Jeannette Rankin and the incredible women who improve their lives through education. So I rallied my friends and neighbors to raise funds for new Jeannette Rankin Foundation scholarships. We raised funds for three awards in just three months time.

My friend, Beth Wagstaff, helped. We created a simple but effective fundraising strategy: we each asked ten people to contribute $50 and find three other people to do the same. We also bolstered support within the community by naming one of the awards in honor of a local woman, Ann Glover Parrott, who has the indominatible spirit of a Jeannette Rankin Foundation woman.

Giving a scholarship in a friend's name is a meaningful way to honor someone who is special. It's very important for us to do things for people while they're here to enjoy it. The positive effects of a Jeannette Rankin Foundation scholarship are like ripples in a pond. Women who receive support from the foundation go on to help their families and give back to their communities.

—Jan Gregory

My story is included in Chapter 5, "Giving Back." Due to an accident, virtually overnight I became disabled, technologically obsolete, and intellectually stagnant. As a single parent, we were living on less than $10,000 a year.

116

With the help of a Jeannette Rankin Foundation scholarship, I earned a Bachelor of Science degree in Communications.

Upon graduation, I began a new career; not long after that, I called JRF with the good news that I had just purchased a home. The former owner, Dorothy Fontana, was recently deceased. In the process of buying the home, I made a special connection with Ms. Fontana's family. They knew that I needed furniture, and they decided to leave the house full of their mother's furnishings to help me! Overwhelmed by their generosity, I wanted to express my gratitude in a meaningful way. I told them about my JRF scholarship, and that I wanted to donate a scholarship in memory of Dorothy Fontana. My gift would help another woman in need with a scholarship, just as I had been helped. Through the Dorothy H. Fontana Award, I provided that gift to a new JRF Scholar.

—Suz Rosenberg Jackson

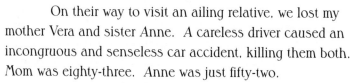

On their way to visit an ailing relative, we lost my mother Vera and sister Anne. A careless driver caused an incongruous and senseless car accident, killing them both. Mom was eighty-three. Anne was just fifty-two.

Among our family and friends, the grief was profound, and the loss was too harsh to accept. Mom and Anne's example of love gave us an option that provided solace amidst our grief. Their compassion and service to others that they generated over their lives was an inheritance – a legacy to preserve. We realized that education had been a silent partner in their lives. Mom used it to birth a childhood dream and became a nurse. Anne used it to reinvent herself as a schoolteacher, and to reaffirm her worth to herself, her family and her community. We decided to give that silent, empowering partner a voice, a presence and a mission.

As it heads into its fourth decade, the Jeannette Rankin Foundation has helped hundreds of women with the same level of desire and determination displayed by Mom and Anne. No other organization speaks the language as clearly and eloquently for a group looking for assistance and affirmation. This is why the Jeannette Rankin Foundation has a new scholarship named the Vera & Anne Purser Award. It is a scholarship that will be given every year in perpetuity. Anne's son Caleb and I donated to the foundation so that other women who need financial assistance will be able to go to college. In Arlington, Virginia, a Giving Circle is providing Anne's book club and friends from the elementary school where she taught an opportunity to help even more women in their quest for a college education. Another Giving Circle launched in Atlanta two years later. The fact that this took time to come to develop echoes the time it takes to pursue an education and to manifest change. For generations to come, women in need will benefit from the generosity of the Jeannette Rankin Foundation while being inspired by the legacy of Mom and Anne. The gift education brings to these hard-working women will allow them to square their shoulders to each day, carry themselves with confidence and share their stories of success with others.

—Michael Purser

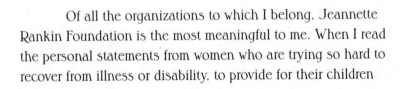

Of all the organizations to which I belong, Jeannette Rankin Foundation is the most meaningful to me. When I read the personal statements from women who are trying so hard to recover from illness or disability, to provide for their children

118

with a good career, to learn a new trade after their factory was shut down, or to break their roots to generations of poverty. I know in my heart the difference that education can make. It doesn't matter that their backgrounds may be so different than mine; it doesn't matter if they live in the city or a rural community, whether they are younger or older than me; what matters is their determination to make a better life for themselves. They can do it.

I see women in my workplace who are steady, responsible workers who are just making ends meet. I encourage them to go back to school to train for better opportunities. They need the courage and the confidence to set new goals and to go after them. It is my hope that they will dare to dream. If they dream, set new goals and go after them with the determination and the grit of Jeannnette Rankin Foundation scholars, the world will open up to them.

A few years ago, I wanted my colleagues at work to get together to pool our resources for a scholarship. It's just the right thing to do. Those of us who are doing alright need to give back to help others in need. It doesn't take that much to make a donation, but it makes a world of difference. I have a party in my home once a year, and I treat my friends to my home cooking – that's something all my friends know is rare. I tell them about the foundation, and the woman who our Giving Circle sponsored the previous year. We all have a good time together, and we donate to renew our scholarship so another woman can have the opportunity to go to college. It's not asking a lot of me or my friends, but it is rewarding to me, far beyond what I give.

—Joyce Waller

afterword

Women Workers Need Education Too!

Anna Quindlen (1997) once noted that women workers "spend their days doing a job most of their co-workers think they can't handle, and then they will go home and do another job most of their co-workers don't want." Her glum portrait sums up the situation of many women in the paid workforce where they must work twice as hard for half as much and simultaneously meet demands of family life. Women have been historically relegated to low-wage, dead-end jobs, particularly when they lack the education to help them gain access to jobs with decent pay and prospects. Breaking this cycle of poverty is challenging and many women lack the resources, moral support, and confidence to succeed.

Over 30 years ago, the visionaries who created the Jeannette Rankin Foundation recognized that women were disadvantaged when it came to educational and occupational opportunities. They realized that women were segregated into low-paying jobs and under-trained. They also believed that education matters for breaking this pattern, but were realistic in their knowledge that non-traditional re-entry women faced myriad challenges in traditional higher education settings, including finding resources to fund higher learning. In spite of these obstacles to women's learning, these visionary founders of the Jeannette Rankin Foundation persisted with the spirit of Jeannette Rankin herself, with the belief that once you educate a woman, you educate a community.

Occupational Segregation

Women have historically been segregated in low-skilled, low-wage jobs where they are paid less than men in almost every country although they work longer hours (AFL-CIO,). Although women compose forty-five percent of the world's workforce, they account for seventy percent of the world's population living in poverty (AFL-CIO,). Women's inter-actions in the workplace are complex, influenced by socialization, identity, family life, socio-economic status, race, sexual orientation, and other variables. These characteristics interact in a system where femaleness is subordinated to the organization culture, industry, geography, politics and history.

Of the 2.8 billion people working in 2003, 1.1 billion were women. Cultural standards dictate women's labor force participation worldwide. Women's family responsibilities have a major impact on the nature of their labor force participation (Davies & Thomas, 2000; Hochschild, 1997; Wilson, 1999) and work roles are gendered where images of the "ideal worker" include aggressiveness, independence, devotion, non-emotion-ality, and rationality.

Women are less likely than men to participate in the workforce in every country for which information is available (Elder & Johnson, 1999). Women's experience of disad-vantage extends across the ranks in organizations. Low paid women are clustered into service sector jobs, which draw lower salaries. Women receive less pay and experience greater rates of unemployment than men worldwide, and often lack the education and training required to secure employment (Elder & Johnson, 1999).

The wage gap has persisted as long as women have been in the paid labor force. Table 1 shows wage gap data on countries for which information was available. In addition to lower rates of pay and higher rates of unemployment, women make up the increasingly contingent part-time workforce.

Women account for well over half of all part-time workers in forty-three countries for which statistics are available (Elder & Johnson, 1999). Low paid or part-time women workers are employed in feminized industries such as banking, nursing, or retail and experience limited opportunity and little incentive to learn and advance. To worsen their situation, these women do not receive health or retirement benefits comparable to full-time workers. If the wage gap closes at the rate it did from 1989 to 2000, it will take over 50 years for women to close the wage gap with men (Caiazza, Shaw & Werschkul, 2003).

Table 1: Average Pay Gap by Country

Country	Gender Pay Gap (%)	Country	Gender Pay Gap (%)
Japan	34.7	Ireland	19.8
Argentina	32.7	Germany	19.4
Korea	26.0	Greece	16.2
Singapore	25.0	Italy	14.3
United Kingdom	24.3	Spain	13.2
United States	24.0	France	10.8
Austria	21.1	Denmark	10.4
Netherlands	21.1	Belgium	7.3
Thailand	20.4	Portugal	5.9

Adapted from ILO (2004) pp. 30-31.

The global labor market is segregated by gender despite the continuing rise of women's participation (Persson & Joung, 1998). Virtually everywhere, women are over-represented in the service sector and underrepresented in the industrial sector. Women made up forty-seven percent of the US workforce in 2003 yet still experience sex segregation in occupations as illustrated in Table 2.

Table 2: 2003 Leading Occupations of Employed Full-time
Wage and Salary Women

%	Occupation
98	Preschool and kindergarten teachers
96	Secretaries/ adminisrative assistants
95	Childcare workers
94	Receptionists and information clerks
93	Registered nurses
93	Teacher assistants
92	Bookkeeping, accounting and auditing clerks
91	Hairdressers, hairstylists, and cosmetologists
91	Nursing, psychiatric, and home health aids
89	Maids and housekeppers

Adapted from US DOL, 2004a

Conversely, women are underrepresented in male-seg-
regated occupations. For instance, women occupy less than
two percent of jobs in construction and from fifteen to nineteen
percent of jobs in manufacturing. Only twenty percent were
first line supervisors, and twenty-one percent were engineers in
2003 (U.S. DOL, 2003b).

Under-trained Workers

Not only are women segregated into low-paying, dead-
end jobs, but also they are undertrained making it difficult to
attain higher paying jobs and prospects. The ILO (1990)
reports that women are excluded from high-profile training
programs thirty-eight percent of the time, yet over thirty-nine
percent of employers regard this state of affairs as a non-issue.
Women and men receive different developmental experiences
in their careers (Federal Glass Ceiling Commission, 1998;
Knoke & Isho, 1998; Ohlott, Ruderman, & McCauley, 1994).

In fact, Still (1985) found that men tend to be sent to training that is promotion-oriented whereas women receive training
for functional skills for their current job. This finding holds
today, where male dominated managerial hierarchies decrease
women's opportunities for career encouragement and training
(Tharenou, Latimer, & Conroy, 1994) and women do not have
equal access to management development programs (Limerick
& Heywood, 1993; Still, 1985). Just as in management,
women tend to become sidelined and marginalized in management education and experiences that would groom them for
ascending the career ladder.

Education Matters!
     If the cycles of gendered job segregation and lack of
access to job training opportunities are to be broken, women
must achieve education. Women's earning power increases significantly with education as evidenced by the following Department of Labor data on earnings with a high school education,
versus two- and four-year degrees. Earning power is increased
almost 60% for all women when comparing a high school
diploma to a 4-year college degree.

Latinas
4 year degree earned a median weekly income of
$676 = $33,800 = 60% increase over HS
2 year degree earned a median weekly income of
$467 = $23,350
H.S. education earned a median weekly income of
$406 = $20,300

African American Women
4 year degree earned a median weekly income of
$692 = $34,600 = 57% increase over HS
2 year degree earned a median weekly income of

$527 = 26.350
H.S. education earned a median weekly income of
$395 = 19.750

White Women
4 year degree earned a median weekly income of
$ 744 = $37.200 61% increase over HS
2 year degree earned a median weekly income of
$579 = $28.950
H.S. education earned a median weekly income of
$ 453 = $22.650

(Department of Labor – 2002 Bureau of Labor statistics)

One of the future trends predicted for higher education by Wise in 1961 was the increasing participation of women over thirty. Statistics substantiate the fact that his prediction was true and suggest that this trend has not yet leveled off. Women now outnumber men in college for the first time since World War II, and it is the increase in the number of women thirty-five and older that accounts for the difference. Women now outnumber men in colleges and universities across the United States, and the growth is among women of "non-traditional" age, that is, older adults.

Reentry is Difficult
The case is clear that educated women have better financial and employment prospects. Yet, women who have been demoralized in the educational system and disadvantaged in the workforce are at a significant disadvantage when it comes to seeking higher education. Returning to school is an intimidating prospect and known as "reentry." Reentry women feel significant angst about returning to school on a college campus where they fear they will not fit in with other learners.

In spite of reentry angst. women overcome it due to their motivation to develop a new career and become self-supporting. Women are also motivated by their families and want to provide better for them financially and set an example for their children. Barriers to reentry can be unsupportive spouses or families and competing family responsibilities.

Reentry women are a good investment. They have been found to have significantly higher grade point averages than do traditional students and reentry men. They also have higher educational aspirations and educational goals than do traditional students. Reentry women have been found to choose social service. education. and health occupations more frequently and do more volunteer work than younger women. (Padula. 2001)

Educate a Woman. and you Educate a Community!

The Jeannette Rankin Foundation was ahead of its time in recognizing the importance of educated women to society. As the stories in this volume attest. when you educate a woman. you also educate her children and her community. Educating women helps end occupational segregation. open up previously unavailable job and occupational training. and increase income.

But more than just improving job and financial prospects. education gives women a sense of pride and confidence that spills over into their families and communities. The knowledge that they will set an example and be able to adequately provide for their families instills a deep sense of achievement and pride that carries forward into the next generation. Educated women give back to their communities and spread their example there as well. Investing in women's education is an investment in everyone's future!

acknowledgments

Daring to Dream would not be a dream come true without the contributions of time, talent and resources of many members of the Jeannette Rankin Foundation community. We would like to extend our heartfelt thanks and deep appreciation to the following: To Tom Payton for encouraging the dream by publishing this work. To Suzi Wong for cultivating the dream through her tireless efforts of interviewing, transcribing and revising scholar interviews. To Heather Kleiner and Susan Bailey for nurturing the dream with their generous financial contributions. To staff members Andrea Anderson, Valerie Lake, Sue Lawrence, and Sue Plaksin for coordinating efforts and supporting the dream from concept to completion. To contributing writers Laura Bierema, Juniper Burrows, Gail Dendy, Mary Erlanger, Jan Gregory, Michael Purser, and Joyce Waller for sharing their experiences and background information. To the foundation's board directors for promoting the dream. To the thirty scholars who opened their life stories to us—they are living the dream. And finally, to all those who support and encourage women succeeding through education by volunteering time, talent, and financial resources. Without you, there would be no dream at all.

editor biographies

Sue Lawrence first became involved with Jeannette Rankin Foundation as a volunteer. She read a personal statement in an application from Emile, who was awarded a JRF Scholarship. Emile's essay painted a vivid portrait of a woman undaunted by limited resources or physical challenges. Sue followed Emile's example of courage and submitted her application to join JRF staff. "I love my work because it is an opportunity to help empower more women toward their goals." Her experience includes management and leadership skills as owner of a graphic design business. She credits her parents for supporting her in college (B.F.A., Wayne State University; M.F.A., Syracuse University) and her friends who have helped her non-traditional path to be one of continual growth, creativity, and dreams.

Suzi Wong believes in the transformative power of education. Her parents, immigrants from China, planted that seed of hope and it has blossomed in her own education (B.A., M.A., M.Ed.), in her career as a teacher, school administrator and advocate for diverse, underserved student populations, and in her current work as gifts officer at the University of Georgia. As Program Coordinator and Student Advisor at the Ban Righ Foundation for Continuing University Education at Queen's University in Canada, she worked with and was inspired by the pluck and promise of non-traditional (or mature) women students returning to school. When she moved to Athens, Georgia, she discovered the Jeannette Rankin Foundation and its mission to help women succeed through education. In sharing the stories of JRF scholarship recipients she not only affirms that mission but also expresses gratitude to all who have helped her in the journey of lifelong learning.

We hope that you have enjoyed reading this book of stories from some amazing women. Their courage and determination is inspiring in light of the challenges they have faced. We now invite you to join in helping more women who dare to dream.

The thread that connects all of the women within this book is that they were selected to receive scholarships from the Jeannette Rankin. Each year, hundreds of qualified women across the United States apply for JRF scholarships toward their dreams of college education. Unlike many other scholarship programs with large endowments, JRF must raise money for its scholarship program plus operating expenses every year.

You can help. A gift from you can help women like Ardella, Carilyn, Marsha, and others go to school. You can be involved in making the difference between poverty and a promising future by making a tax-deductible donation to Jeannette Rankin Foundation. Contributions in any amount are sincerely appreciated. You may make a copy of the form below and mail it, or make a donation online by visiting www.rankinfoundation.org.

[ ] Yes! I wish to help women like Ardella, Carilyn, Marsha and others toward their dreams of a college education.

[ ] Enclosed is a check for my gift of $_____ to support the Jeannette Rankin Foundation program.
Please charge $_____ to my   MasterCard [ ]   Visa [ ]

[ ] I wish to make a recurring donation. Please charge my card monthly in the amount of $_____   MasterCard [ ]   Visa [ ]

[ ] I am interested in making a significant investment in the success of women and their families. Please contact me.
Name_____
Address_____
City, State, Zip_____
Phone_____

Email_____

[ ] Please make my gift in honor of (name)_____

[ ] Please send a card to
Name_____
Address_____
City, State, Zip_____